I0096726

The Trumpster Fire Escape Almanac

Facts to Plan Your Expat Life

By Thomas Pained

Copyright © 2025 Thomas Pained

All rights reserved. No part of this publication may be reproduced, distributed, or transmitted in any form or by any means, including photocopying, recording, or other electronic or mechanical methods, without the prior written permission of the publisher, except in the case of brief quotations embodied in critical reviews and certain other noncommercial uses permitted by copyright law. Any perceived slight against any individual is purely unintentional.

Although the author and publisher have made every effort to ensure that the information in this book was correct at press time, the author and publisher do not assume and hereby disclaim any liability to any party for any loss, damage, or disruption caused by errors or omissions, whether such errors or omissions result from negligence, accident, or any other cause. The content of this book is for entertainment purposes only. Neither author nor publisher accepts any responsibility for the results of any actions taken on the basis of information in this book. Author and publisher expressly disclaim all and any liability and responsibility to any person in respect of the consequences of anything done or omitted to be done by such person in reliance, whether wholly or partially, upon this book.

For permission requests, write to the publisher at contact@identitypublications.com.

ISBN-13: 978-1-969995-06-4 (paperback)
ISBN-13: 978-1-945884-98-6 (hardcover)
ISBN-13: 978-1-945884-99-3 (ebook)
ISBN-13: 978-1-969995-00-2 (audiobook)

First edition, published by Identity Publications.

CONTENTS

Preface v

Chapter 1: Is an Expatriate an Ex-Patriot? 1

Chapter 2: What Tint Is Your Target? 5

Chapter 3: The Statistics 21

Chapter 4: Your Scouting Visit. 69

Chapter 5: When You Like What You See 77

Conclusion 85

Appendix 89

Preface

"Has someone made smoke in the house? If it's not too bad, I'll stay. If it's too much, I'll leave. For you must always remember and hold fast to this, that the door is open."

— Epictetus, 1st Century CE

Being, as it is, an almanac, this is a book full of facts and statistics, but it's also an escape manual, so perhaps it's not out of place to remind ourselves a bit about the Trumpster Fire we're living in.

How did these news items make you feel?

- A foreign graduate student studying legally in the US was arrested by masked FBI agents on a public street because she had peacefully expressed positions that differed with policies of the current Administration. The President assured us that this and similar arrests are "the first of many."

- Tens of thousands of Federal employees were discharged at the behest of the richest man in the world, unelected and uninformed about the duties of the employees or their departments broadly. He takes mad pleasure in swinging a chainsaw around in public.

▸ The stock market has been whipsawed by a tariff policy that changes daily, with the President even dropping hints about when to buy and sell stocks. The on-and-off tariff rates are based on a bizarre, simple, one-fits-all formula. The value of the dollar is dropping *vis-à-vis* other world currencies. At the same time, extremely poor countries are being made to suffer.

▸ The Secretary of Education was invited to participate in a panel discussion of Artificial Intelligence in Education and repeatedly referred to it as "A-One" instead of "A-Eye."

▸ When an interviewer asked the President in the Oval Office what the Declaration of Independence means—a document about revolution and separation—he responded, "Peace and Unity," as if the Continentals were cordially invited to the Hessians' Christmas Party on December 25, 1776.

Honestly, I cut this list off at the beginning of May 2025, before leaving for a trip to scout for a new homeland. I recently returned to the US after two months away. A week or so ago, I walked down Wilshire Boulevard in Los Angeles and was told that it was full of soldiers not long before. And a friend told me yesterday that the scene was being repeated in Washington now. If I read everything that's happened since April to glean new items for my list, I'm pretty sure that I'd be too profoundly depressed to finish writing this book.

Are you angry? After more than ten years of constant media exposure to the dangerous political clown Donald Trump—

accompanied in the clown car by the entire Republican Party——
the quip is now that "Canada is like a really nice condo above a
meth lab." Many people feel that the United States of America
reached a genuine historical turning point in November 2024,
even a breaking point.

I had always planned a stint overseas during retirement
at some indefinite time. But not long ago, I realized I was
experiencing anger not just when I read the news, but when I
walked down the streets of the seat of the rural county where I
live. My county broke 62-38 for Trump in 2024. Everyone I pass
(at least every white person) makes me think: *I bet you voted for
him!* Many Trump voters are now saying: *Yes, but I didn't vote for
this!* Dude, it was all spread out in front of you beforehand. So
now you've decided to wake up and smell the… coffee.

Add to that that I've been thinking of buying a gun,
something I couldn't have imagined needing before 2020. I'm
afraid of anyone who could vote for a candidate whose platform
was planked with various forms of meanness to others, wrapped
in the American and Christian flags.

*This anger is not good for my health. It's not good for yours,
either.*

If you're not familiar with that quote from Epictetus, well,
I myself made it through six decades without ever hearing of
the bloke. But if you *are* familiar with it, you will know that he
refers to *The Big Door*: suicide. Fortunately, there is a different
door for those of us choking on Trumpster Fire smoke. We can
vote with our feet and leave the USA—if not indefinitely, at
least until the fire is put out. We are welcome in many other
countries. And hold fast to this: the door we're talking about
is *open in both directions!* The USA is always just a plane ride or
two away.

When I tell friends and acquaintances of my plans, so many of the reactions are along the lines of:

- *I wish I could do that. But… the language, my grandchildren, my spouse, my job, my finances, my health, my kids' school…*
- *We're an infertile couple. We're scared that IVF could be restricted or even become a crime. We'd like to go somewhere to be sure of infertility treatment. And we have friends who had successful treatment and still have embryos in the freezer. They're afraid of being charged with an illegal abortion if they dispose of the embryos. But… will we really be welcome?*
- *I'm worried; Like you, I don't like guns in the house, but my spouse insisted that we buy one after January 6, and it makes me feel even more anxious. But… is it safe where* you're *going to go?*
- *I'd like to leave. But… I'd feel guilty for abandoning my country.*

All of these are legitimate concerns, and for some, there may be insurmountable obstacles of various sorts, such as taking care of infirm family members.[1] But for many others, the "obstacles" may be imaginary. For example, it's easy to keep in touch. You can call your little brother for free from almost anywhere on WhatsApp—whereas when I was in college in the 1970s, I paid the equivalent of $2 per minute to call Mom on the other side of my home state, sometimes to ask for money to pay my phone bill. That notion of "abandonment" will be the first item of discussion in Chapter 1.

---

1   *Your expat foothold in another country might even be an escape for family members in the future.*

This book is not a travel guidebook or tourist brochure. I will not be describing any of Lamai, Sydney, or The Algarve as having "one of the best white/black sand beaches in the world, bathed in the warm South China Sea/Mediterranean/Pacific sun." When you have homed in on a country or two, you can buy your Fodor's or Lonely Planet or Conde Nast or Rough Guide, or you can just dive into an internet rabbit hole.

If you want to act instead of dream and fret, you must complete two tasks.

The first task is to take an inventory of your situation, your needs, and your desires, that is, to be clear about what you are looking for. If you just go to an exotic beach and "fall in love" and only then look into how to move, it's likely to turn out like a lot of beach resort romances. An experienced coastal real estate agent once told me, "In the business we say, 'They just have sand in their shoes.'" In Part I, we'll embark on taking that inventory.

Part II is an almanac with facts and figures for a long but curated list of destinations: weather, democratic institutions, economic development, expat community, language, and presence of English speakers, etc. The information is compiled from more than a dozen reliable sources, like the World Bank, *World Population Review, The CIA Factbook, The Economist,* and official government websites. My intention is to present you with facts and figures that will help you make a practical choice. You should not make a permanent move without a visit, but the contents of this book should point you in the right direction, or at least some workable directions. Then you can plan your scouting visit or visits. It's true: some people *do* fall in love with a place they're visiting and never go home. And it makes a great magazine story. I suspect these people have no responsibilities. For the rest of us, it's important to perform efficient due diligence, and a look at *The Trumpster Fire Escape Almanac* is where to start.

The third step, of course, is to make a scouting visit (or two) to your best candidates. Part III offers some suggestions on the nitty-gritty: health insurance, taxes, visas and passports, and similar issues. It's not feasible to compile a list of, say, visa requirements for every country cited in the statistical table. I will address the topics generally, and there is a list of selected written resources.

Part IV is for *you* to write: Investigate and visit one or more potential destinations, select your new life, and go on your new journey and be happy!

A personal—and personal-pronoun—note: This is a special almanac about your journey and mine, not *The Information, Please Almanac* or *The CIA World Factbook.* I've freely written about "you" and "me," rather always keeping distance in the third person or passive voice. It really is about me—I gathered these statistics for myself. I'm sharing the fruit of an uncommon skill with you—I'm a data scientist. As I write these words, I am still living in the US, but I just returned from a visit to two candidate countries. I visited two others in 2019 and 2022.

I've made my decision and have begun working on my visa application for the country I've chosen. I will not be tipping my hand about which country. However, I do cite Guatemala as an example frequently. Let me explain that I've spent around six months in Guatemala over the past three years doing volunteer work, so I'm, relatively speaking, knowledgeable about the country. I know many comfortable, happy expats there. My comments about Guatemala (or any other country) are just examples and are not meant to be either encouraging or discouraging. I will tip my hand enough to say that I will continue to volunteer there every year, but I will not move there. I will get moving to "Mysteria." At least one-third of the net proceeds from selling this book will be used to support the charity I co-founded there.

"Thomas Pained" is a pseudonym, like "Poor Richard." Senator Lisa Murkowski, Republican of Alaska, stated recently that "Retaliation is real." The un-presidential threat to deport US citizens can't be taken lightly. For this reason, I also don't name the charity I'll mention more than once.

Good luck on your voyage to a happier, smoke-free life!

DISCLAIMER

You should rely on this book only to screen locations for your new home, not to make your ultimate decision about expatriation! (You know this, right?)

I've made best efforts to present accurate and useful facts in this book. There were a lot of ways to make a mistake: choosing an unreliable dataset, misinterpreting a reliable dataset, making an error writing the computer programs that compile and analyze the data, or just saying something stupid that I thought was true. It's not possible to verify every cell in the tables and spreadsheets.

But it's my book, and no one else is to blame for the inevitable errors!

Nothing in this book is intended to disparage anyone except Trump voters. Nothing is intended to disparage any country mentioned.

CHAPTER 1

Is an Expatriate an Ex-Patriot?

"Those who gave up essential liberty to purchase eggs cheaply deserve neither liberty nor eggs."[2]

— Benjamin Franklin, 2025

There are many different factors to consider when deciding where your best expat life would be, and, of course, whether you will even have one. There are lots of possible motivations for expatriation besides fear and loathing of Trumpism and a foreboding sense that our Republic is coming to an end: adventure, economic opportunities, family overseas, or you're hoping to avoid future sedition charges from your Facebook

---

[2] *"They who can give up essential liberty to purchase a little temporary safety, deserve neither liberty nor safety"*
Benjamin Franklin, 1755.

posts. But most readers will have this question of principle on their mind: *Is an expatriate an ex-patriot?* You must search your soul about that before searching your soul to put together a wish list for your new home.

You may be apolitical. You may just want to move abroad to *be* apolitical—to get the tumultuous political noise out of your ears. Although I donate significantly to a small number of political causes every year, I try to avoid being constantly upset by things I can't control. I confine news media to one day a week, and I unsubscribed from political mailing lists—or tried to.

Nonetheless, some friends I've talked to aren't apolitical, and they feel some sense of guilt about considering a move abroad:

▸ *Is it wrong to leave instead of staying and fighting?*
▸ *Am I abandoning my country when it needs me?*
▸ *If I leave, will I have a clear conscience?*
▸ *Can I leave my country permanently and still say I love it?*

These are questions that no one else can answer for you. But did you hold fast to this? *The expat door is two-way*, and home is almost always just a plane ticket away. Probably a better question is:

▸ *Can I leave my country temporarily and still say I love it?*

Let's talk about two patriots you've probably heard of. One is "The First American": Benjamin Franklin; the other, "The Father of the American Revolution": Thomas Paine. Both signed the Declaration of Independence on July 4, 1776.

The Continental Congress dispatched Benjamin Franklin to France in 1777, and he was still there when the British surrendered at Yorktown in October 1781. Thomas Paine joined him early in 1781. It is quite likely that they often dined richly in Paris while Washington's Army was barely dining at all. (In fact, Ben is frequently described as a *"bon vivant."*) But they showed their love of country by leaving home to persuade the King of France to support the American cause, including with the naval support that clinched the Battle of Yorktown. After the Revolution, Paine returned to France for several years and was appointed by France's revolutionary government to assist in drafting a constitution, transmitting at least some new American values to the French.

What will you do to fight Trumpism and MAGA if you stay, anyway? Be honest: Write down what you *will do*, not what you *could* do or *might* do if you're not busy that Saturday. That might include:

- Attending peaceful protest rallies.
- Canvassing door to door.
- Boycotting Tesla.
- Donating money to political candidates' campaigns.
- Donating money to activist groups such as the ACLU.
- Donating money to medical research activities that are suffering from budget cuts.
- Participating in phone banks.
- Calling your senator, or congressperson, or the White House.

Let's look at this carefully. Yes, you have to be Stateside for rallies and door-to-door canvassing, but consider what you can do abroad:

- You can forgo Teslas and Target shopping anywhere, if you want to.

- You can donate money online from anywhere in the world with your credit card. (If you're living in a less expensive country, you can donate even more with some of that windfall.)
- You can call potential voters and legislators from anywhere on your cell phone. If the calls are not free, they will be cheap.
- Finally, you can let your friends in your new expat home know that we're not all MAGgots. (Maybe you can hand out copies of Paine's *Common Sense*.)

If you're not currently making donations or phone calls, I'm not suggesting that you have to start. But you *can* still participate in politics or support de-subsidized charities if you wish.

There are lots of reasons you might need to stay put, but guilt about lack of patriotism shouldn't be one of them. Think about it: Most Trump voters are going to stick around and do nothing to save their country. If you work on that list above in a significant way from abroad, you'll be doing more to save your country than at least half of your compatriots.

If you are still struggling with this, do what a therapist would tell you to do in any bad relationship: Make two columns on a sheet of paper and write down "Reasons to Stay" and "Reasons to Leave." You might end up feeling like staying in this mess is no different than "staying together for the kids," and it's really just one of many factors to consider. If you move abroad, there is a lot of unpleasant uncertainty, just like leaving a marriage. But you can always get back together with this "spouse," unlike the human sort, and you'll have a chance to fall in love with someplace new—or at least have an exciting "affair" with your new place of residence.

CHAPTER 2

What Tint Is Your Target?

"You can't be a country without a beer and an airline. It helps if you have some kind of football team… but at the very least, you need a beer."

— Frank Zappa
American Musician, 1940–1993

It's time to work out what is on your wish list and need list. I advise you to write down all the questions this chapter raises in your mind. Then write your answers to the questions. That can keep you focused. If "you" is plural, consider doing this separately so that you aren't giving answers to please your partner, and only then get together to make the compromises you need to make. If "you" is singular, find a friend who might tell you things that you need to know about yourself during this process. (It might not hurt to bring your friend along when you travel to countries on your short list!)

FORM OF GOVERNMENT

I assume you're not interested in jumping from the frying pan of what *The Economist* rated a "flawed democracy" even pre-Trump into the fire of what it calls an "authoritarian regime." If you have family or other reasons to want to move to an authoritarian country, this almanac won't be of much use to you. On the other hand, there is a middle ground called "hybrid regimes," which includes Mexico, for example, where 26% of all US expats live. (In 2024, the United States was nestled in the democracy rankings between France and Chile, by the way.)

Here are some examples in each category. I have deliberately chosen some less familiar countries.

Full democracies include the Netherlands, Costa Rica, Uruguay, Portugal, and Greece. Of all US expats, 39% live in full democracies.

Flawed democracies include the US, Belgium, Panama, Thailand, South Korea, and the Dominican Republic. 16% of US expats live in flawed democracies (as well as 100% of US residents).

Hybrid regimes include those of Guatemala, Mexico, Romania, Ecuador, and Panamá. 33% of US expats live in these countries—but recall that 26% of all expats live in Mexico alone.

As Leo Tolstoy wrote in the first line of *Anna Karenina* (and the last line I've read, honestly) "All happy families are alike; every unhappy family is unhappy in its own way." The same is true of hybrid governments. Each is unhappy in its own ways. It would be a good idea to investigate those ways in some detail if you plan to reside in a place with a hybrid government. (Rigged elections are bad, but maybe better than jailed journalists.) It's not possible for me to describe all unhappy governments in detail.

What about participating in political activities where you are living? If you enjoy moderate stimulation from observing the push-and-pull of sane politics, you might enjoy keeping tabs on the local scene. You won't have such a big emotional stake, so you might not find it gut-wrenching. Certainly, if you live in one of the full democracies, you can express your opinion openly (and peacefully) as a foreigner. As we slide further down the scale of democracy, the dangers increase. When Guatemala freely elected a new president in 2020, passing a law to expel NGOs like Human Rights Watch that "disturb the public order" was at the top of the agenda.[3] In some countries, it may be acceptable to campaign for causes, but, really, until and unless you gain citizenship, is it any of your business what candidates citizens elect?

Also remember: If you express opinions about local politics, you are opening yourself up to questions about American politics, and then you're back staring at the flames of the Trumpster Fire. (Once burnt, twice shy?) You may even encounter some Trump admirers. Personally, I don't want to have those conversations.

LANGUAGE

How do you feel about learning a new language? Great news! Moving to a new country can give you a chance to take pride in acquiring a new skill!

But I barely made it through my foreign language requirement in college! Señora Jones and I hated each other!

Language pedagogy has made a lot of advances since I started college in the 1970s. The predominant model of

---

3   *His party was voted out of office in 2024 despite a lot of chicanery.*

instruction then was the so-called "Audio-Lingual Method." I had lectures to explain grammar for an hour a week. Then we "practiced speaking" in small recitation classes three hours a week. But "recitation" was a TA repeatedly circling the room, asking the whole class and individual students to, for example, change a sentence in the perfect tense to the pluperfect tense. Studies eventually estimated that students' frustration about not learning how to carry on a conversation stemmed from the fact that *they averaged less than a minute a week in conversation!*

If that's what you remember, you're in for a surprise. In 2025, language-learning apps like Duolingo[4] are fun and get you moving quickly. Put this book down and spend 15 minutes with Duolingo. You will get constant feedback, and you can repeat as much as you wish. There are 30-second multimedia flashcards for speaking, listening, reading, and writing. The apps use "spaced repetition"—if you miss a question, it goes back into the deck of interactive flashcards, and you will see it again later. The audio is recorded by native speakers, and you can record phrases in your own voice for correction by the app. But if you put, say, ten hours into it and really aren't getting anywhere, you can fail early in the US and proceed to Plan B. How many Ellis Islanders had such an opportunity?

If you decide to attend a language school either in the US or abroad, more good news! ALM was replaced long ago by "Language in Context," which emphasizes conversations among students in small groups. You can expect this if you

---

4   *Since 35,000 expats are already living in Brazil and Portugal... Heads up! The pronunciation of Brazilian Portuguese and "Portuguese Portuguese" are so different that Boston hospitals employ two sets of interpreters. Look for apps and websites waving the colors of the correct national flag. If there's no flag, it's probably Brazilian (like DuoLingo.)*

study in a good language school at home or abroad. And there are many opportunities for affordable online instruction with teachers around the world.

But... doesn't English cover the Earth, like Sherwin-Williams? According to Wikipedia, English is an official language in 29 countries in our country table. You are likely familiar with South Africa, Jamaica, Ireland, and New Zealand. You might be surprised by Malta, Ghana, Kenya, Tanzania, the Philippines, and Singapore. However, not *everyone* speaks English even in every one of these countries.

- In African villages in former English colonies, many children don't learn English until they go to school, and not everyone has attended school.
- In the EU, English instruction is nearly universal, and it's widely used in commerce and higher education. English, we might say, is Europe's new Latin. But even so, many do not speak competent English.
- In Latin America, English is official only in Belize and Guyana. (It's not correct to call them "Latin American," in fact.) Generally, English skills are not great but improving.
- Good English is hard to come by in Southeast Asia, except in the Philippines, Singapore, and Hong Kong, and in tourist areas.

Of course, there's Google Translate. But you and your conversational partner will both feel better about yourselves if you try to speak a little of the language. Trust me—I recently got a round of applause from a couple of hundred indigenous people just by saying "Greetings to y'all!" in their language. And we are all familiar with agitation in the US against people who "don't even learn the language," fair or not. It's not uniquely American. Be a good neighbor and show the natives of your new country that you admire their culture and traditions. Make language learning a priority.

YOUR STANDARD OF LIVING

Whether you are a retiree, a digital nomad, or a jobseeker, you will want to think about your new standard of living—relative to your current one, of course, but also relative to the people around you.

According to Numbeo (numbeo.com), living in Switzerland costs 40% more than living in the US. But we know that cost of living varies widely in the United States, especially housing, and likewise in other countries. If you move from Topeka to Zurich, you will have a hard time matching your current living standard without finding matching employment in Zurich. If you move to Guanajuato, Mexico, a large increase in your standard of living will be possible, since it costs half as much there as in the US.

In fact, other than some Caribbean islands, only three countries are more expensive than the US, so if a substantial part of your income is passive or you fill a US job remotely, you have a whole range of options to improve your standard of living.

You've no doubt heard—or experienced—that "a dollar's worth a lot more there." Table I includes estimates of the purchasing power of a dollar based on World Bank statistics— but to fill a market basket of *local* products that satisfy a uniform definition of adequacy. If you want to buy what's in your current *US* market basket rather than substituting equivalent products locals use to meet the same needs, you will reduce or erase your gain in purchasing power. The market basket doesn't always include imported goods like cars, electronics, and gas. They are typically subject to significant tariffs in middle- and lower-income countries. And of course, costs of living vary *within* every country. Are you willing to give up some American-style products and replace them with local substitutes? Some have found that this naturally leads to a healthier diet.

Finally, the dollar has been slipping recently versus gold and the euro and other currencies, diminishing the dollar's purchasing power abroad. Many talking heads and scammers claim to know what will happen in the future. I don't. But I will say more about purchasing power in our statistical tables.

LOCAL STANDARD OF LIVING

What about how the residents of the country live? If you belong to America's middle class, your standard of living could be considered upper class in Latin American countries or parts of Asia. We can certainly observe poverty and homelessness in the United States, but many of us don't walk by it when we go down the street. It is more widespread, more extreme, and more visible in some other countries. In countries where you might regard much of the middle class as poor, and the houses of the poor might look like shacks, how will you feel? (The true answer is that you won't know until you visit, but it still deserves thought now. I recommend a meaningful visit to a poor country sometime, even if you don't intend to settle there. Volunteer for a week or two!)

Will you seek out the highest standard of living you can afford, or will you seek to live as you do now and save money—or somewhere in between? Or do you see this as a chance to simplify? If you are living in Western Europe, where standards are similar, you will probably feel comfortable with local living standards, but in popular retirement destinations like Ecuador or Thailand, you could feel differently.

EXPATS? SENIORS? TOURISTS?

According to *World Population Review*, there are 3.1 million non-military Americans living abroad, 2.6 million in our list of democracies. Twenty-seven percent live in Mexico; 9% in Canada. Although balanced overall, the ratio of males to females varies from country to country in surprising ways: 1.24 in Greece; 0.78 in Germany.

Certainly, you can enjoy the company of other English speakers if you connect yourself to a community of expats. One option for expat retirees is a gated community with a clubhouse with pickleball courts and a weekly bridge club meeting—or even something like the Gringolandia neighborhood in Cuenca, Ecuador, where an estimated 10 to 15 thousand North Americans live. Or you can live in a small town where you may be the subject of curiosity and attention, hopefully friendly. Or you can build an isolated house on a mountainside. Or live among locals in a cosmopolis filled with museums and well-groomed parks. Wherever you live, you will probably appreciate some support from the expat community in your country. There are undoubtedly social media groups for expats, probably including some locals who like to help (and/or sell real estate and legal services to) expats.

How do you feel about tourists? There are locations in most countries that are full of local and international tourists. There's a colonial town I have visited repeatedly during my travels, and I enjoy sitting in the town square offering to take pictures of tourists for a couple of hours sometimes, but I don't want to do that night after night, and I'm happy to re-immerse myself in the Spanish language when I leave town. Frankly, the behavior of many tourists is embarrassing. One of the cringiest, most appalling moments of my recent years was in a minibus full of young single marketing specialists in Guatemala. We were stranded for an hour in front of a poor family's house—a shack, really—with the kids out front watching us from the stoop to pass their time. My bus-mates were busy comparing the miles and rebates on their credit cards.

In tourist areas, you'll have opportunities to "practice" your English with tourists from North America, Europe, and elsewhere. Depending on your status (or aversion to legal jeopardy), you may be able to create a part-time gig helping them out in one way or another.

Do you want to mix with fellow seniors—or are you a younger person who wants to mop up the wisdom we excrete whenever we sit on a barstool? The senior population may interest you, and that is reported in my tables.

MEDICAL CARE

Do you have unique health concerns, or just general concerns? The quality of medical care is a concern for everyone. Most European countries have great healthcare systems, but you may not get much love with a tourist visa. For example, if you have a retiree's visa for Ireland, you will have to show proof of private health insurance, and you cannot receive any other government benefits, either. If you are in Guatemala, a situation of any gravity is likely to require a medical evacuation. Some countries further down the income scale have medical systems as good or better than the US's. Wherever you go, you should be sure about how you will pay for any maintenance meds, and whether they are approved and readily available. The retail price is certain to be cheaper than where you live now! Many countries will require you to use private medical facilities or pay upfront for services at a public provider. *Whenever* you are abroad, it's important to be sure you have health coverage. (Don't make assumptions. Ask questions.) Reasonably priced private insurance is usually available. Many locals prefer to use private facilities, even in some Western European countries.

CLIMATE

Climate is certainly very important to me personally. I've been constrained to live in a place with very hot, humid, long summers for many years, shvitzing like a shmedrick. I'm looking for a cool home near or in the mountains. I'm sure you have your own ideas. What will be desirable or at least acceptable to you? Snow or not? Year-round beach? Can you deal with a short but intense rainy season? Heat? Will you personally need air conditioning or central heating, and is it generally available? Most of us know more about the climate in American cities than elsewhere. It will probably be helpful to write down *American* cities with your desirable and acceptable climates. The tables can help you find cities with the same climate classification. Weatherspark.com will generate detailed graphical year-round comparisons of two or more cities.

CRIME AND SAFETY

When I told an old friend a couple of years ago that I was going to Guatemala for a couple of months, she told me with some certainty, "*You won't come back alive! You'll be killed by the gangs!*"[5] I think she honestly thought I should pack my clothes in a body bag.

Central American gang murders are what we hear about, and of course, they are real. The current US administration *loves* to amplify dramatic (and sometimes manufactured) stories to convince us that all Spanish-speaking brown people need to be forcibly expelled. In 2023, the US homicide rate was 5.6 per 100,000, the tenth highest in the world, but then, there are 20% more civilian firearms than people, nearly twice as many as any other country. The guns are mostly in the hands of US citizens, not Mexican rapists. The 2024 murder rate in Guatemala was 16.1—almost three times as high, with only a tenth of the guns. So, should you feel safer in peaceful Indianapolis? The homicide rate in Nap Town was *50% higher than Guatemala's!* It's important to know where *not* to spend your time in any country. You probably already know not to go camping near the 541-mile-long Mexico-Guatemala border. You should also avoid Tuxedo Park in Indianapolis.

If you are concerned about mass shootings, in the period 2000 to 2022, the Rockefeller Institute recorded 109 mass shootings in the US and 62 in all other countries put together. (Mass shooting definitions and statistics are contentious. I'm not going there.) It's important to bear in mind that mass shooting deaths are extremely rare even in the United States. On the other hand, if school shootings are an ongoing source of anxiety for your children, an escape overseas could provide relief.

---

5   *Sadly, my friend assumed a bigger risk than I did. Because she had no insurance, she ignored warning signs of cancer until she went on Medicare at 65. She didn't make it much beyond enrollment.*

Perhaps you'd like to move someplace even safer, and that's perfectly reasonable. But maintain perspective and don't dismiss countries solely according to national crime statistics or highly publicized cases.

Another kind of safety is traffic safety. Among the 99 countries in our list for which statistics were readily available, the US ranked in the middle for traffic deaths with 13 per 100,000 population, almost the same as Mexico. Nearly every country with a lower rate is European and has well-developed public transport. Aside from the Dominican Republic (65), no country's rate exceeds 40. As an expat, you can easily avoid much of the risk that locals assume. For example, you will not fail to fasten your seatbelt, nor will you put a family of four on a motorcycle with no helmets. If you walk where there are no sidewalks, you will not walk with your back to traffic. These are all standard procedures in Guatemala, though, where the rate is 23 deaths per 100,000, but not in neighboring Honduras, where the rate is only 16.

FLYING FROM AND TO THE US

Most likely, you'll want to see family and friends on holidays and other occasions. You need to consider money and time costs. The same applies to your visitors. You might be flying college students to your new home for the summer. In terms of money costs, it's no secret that airlines practice "dynamic pricing," so it's hard to know how much you'll need to pay for a ticket from one day to the next. (On the other hand, the ideas that you should clear cookies or buy in the wee hours on Tuesday have been debunked. This pointless BS wouldn't help an airline's bottom line, so they don't bother.)

I currently live within three hours of two major hubs. It's now late April 2025. I can fly one way to Thailand on Monday, June 23 for $850, to Portugal for $500, to Uruguay for $500, to Costa Rica for $150, to Australia for $900, to South Africa for $1,000, and to Panama for $200. I didn't search on other days or for round-trips to find the cheapest flights. In 1978, I paid the equivalent of $3,500 to fly to Europe on Icelandic—the *bargain* airline. Flights are not free, but they are more affordable than ever, even without looking hard. (It turns out that airlines now take in a large share of their revenues by selling frequent-flyer miles to credit card companies. Fares are secondary.) If your US visits are flexible, be sure to enroll in all the frequent-flyer programs and keep an eye out for bargains arriving in your email or set alerts on sites like Kayak for routes that interest you.

EDUCATION

I suspect only a small fraction of my readers are concerned with educating children, and it's not feasible to describe education systems that vary so widely (if not wildly) in organization and quality around the world. It seemed to be hard work to find the right school for my kids, even in the single large public school system available to us. I'm afraid you have a lot of homework if schools are among your needs. If you want to have your children educated in English in a non-English-speaking country, you can expect to pay for private schools. These, too, vary in quality and price.

PLANES, TRAINS, AND AUTOMOBILES

The US is famous for its lack of public transportation, but in countries where a smaller fraction of the population owns cars, it is necessary and widely available. Will you want a car? Do you like the train? Do you savor airline coffee? How about the bus? Do you *need* a car for transportation, or is it more of a security blanket? You might have some good reasons for acquiring a car, but trying to go without one could give you a chance to collect your reasons.

Most large cities around the world are served by buses, streetcars, or light rail. Taxis are available practically everywhere, and Uber (or Bolt or Lyft) is now available in many countries, at least in larger cities. Although trains exist in many parts of the world, they cannot compete with airlines over longer distances in large or sparsely populated countries (such as the United States.) In countries with economies based on exploitation of natural resources, any railroads may have originally been laid to transport coal or ores to ports rather than to provide passenger services, and they may have been abandoned even for freight service as roads and vehicles have improved. (Quetzaltenango in Guatemala had the first electric railroad in Latin America. You can still see the rails—being used as lampposts and guard rails.) A long rail or bus trip can be a good way to become familiar with a country's landscapes, but you may not want to repeat it.

Europe's trains have always been legendary, including high-speed rail on many intercity routes, but I discovered that buses can be faster, even between national capitals. Cheap flights are now available. If you reside in the Schengen Zone, you will be able to travel freely around Europe without additional formalities. Cities are well-served by buses, streetcars, and taxis.

Trains barely exist in Latin America, but comfortable modern intercity buses serve most countries. At the risk of sounding snobby, I'll opine that these buses typically carry a more respectable clientele than US intercity buses, simply because having no car itself is more respectable. Various other types of buses provide service over shorter distances at varying levels of comfort, including minibuses and recycled American school buses (like Guatemala's famous "chicken buses.") You may get a more comfortable but still reasonably priced ride by contacting a tour company and tagging along in a bus full of backpackers or day-tripping tourists.

Many bigger Latin American cities have efficient bus systems and often light rail or designated priority lanes and routes for buses—sometimes even aerial tramways serving neighborhoods on mountainsides. Smaller towns are typically served taxis, moto-taxis ("tuctucs"), and even aerial tramways in some Andean cities.

In Africa, some countries have passenger rail service, but they are not very practical beyond relatively short distances.

Asian countries like Taiwan, South Korea, and Japan are well served by trains. Taiwan's high-speed rail is competitive with airplanes, once time for clearing security is taken into account. In countries in archipelagos like Japan or Indonesia, rail and road routes may include ferries, making them yet slower relative to air travel. Thailand and India have extensive railroad systems, but speed, safety, and comfort are sometimes lacking.

Australia's state capitals, formerly served by railroads of three different gauges, have been joined by standard gauge tracks since the early 21st Century. Australia's population is sparse, and passenger service is correspondingly sparse. According to Rome2Rio, train trips across Australia from Perth to Sydney and across the US from San Francisco to New York City each take about 74 hours. Driving either route takes 40–45 hours.

The website Rome2Rio (www.rome2rio.com) is a great way to explore every means of transportation by entering departure and destination cities. It's a good way to explore your options in general terms, and I was surprised to find that the schedules were generally reliable during my recent travels in Europe and Latin America.

RECREATION

How do you entertain yourself? Do you want to continue, or try new things? How will you acquire supplies for your 3D printer? Do you like historical sites?

Is there good skiing? Don't assume that countries lying between the Tropic of Capricorn and the Tropic of Cancer don't have winter sports. It is, in fact, possible to ski *on the line of the Equator* on Cayambe Volcano in Ecuador, although there are no lifts anywhere in the country. It is also possible to waterski in Frenchman Lake in the Yukon.

Do you play cards? Euchre is not widely played outside the Great Lakes region of the US and Canada, but I have played in the jungle in Guatemala with expats from Ontario and Illinois.

Electronics and technology can be significantly more expensive in some countries, impacting hobbies such as woodworking, 3D printing, sound equipment and musical instruments, and drones. If you want to take your expensive tools, some countries allow a single shipment duty-free when you become a resident.

It's likely that you can find most activities in most countries if you try, but if you have important special interests, you should probably get on those expat Facebook groups and look before you leap. The one hobby that may be difficult to practice in some countries is hunting.

CHAPTER 3

The Statistics

"Ninety-five percent of statistical jokes are stale."

— Unknown

SOME FACTS ABOUT COLLECTING FACTS

Part II is devoted to "the numbers." It included two large tables—spreadsheets—loaded with statistics. Table I has a row for each of 99 countries. Table II has a row for nearly 500 cities in those countries. (My downloadable spreadsheet has many more than can be printed feasibly in a book, and I expect to add more data items, so please visit www.thompained.com and add your name to my mailing list to be informed of updates) Almost all data comes either from downloaded spreadsheets or from "scraping" the World Wide Web. (This generally means downloading the HTML encoding of the webpages and using specialized software to pull out the good stuff and put it into spreadsheets.)

Most statistics are drawn from sources that are widely regarded as reliable, such as the World Bank, the United Nations, and international weather databases. I have tried to use reliable statistics and give my caveats when it seemed appropriate. It's obviously not possible to check every cell of the spreadsheet.

Statistics that rely only on measurements are *primary statistics*. Of course, primary statistics such as population can be estimates or may be collected in different years in different countries, for example, in censuses. Since I don't expect my readers to conduct further statistical analyses or base academic papers on my tables, I am content to include representative statistics less than five years old, even if not from the same year.

Other statistics are *derivative* statistics, such as *The Economist's* scoring of democratic institutions. A derivative statistic is a weighted score of primary statistics, just as the numeric score on an exam at school is a weighted average of the scores of the individual questions. We've all felt that certain questions didn't measure mastery of the subject, or that a certain question was overweighted. It's no different for a single score for democracy, safety, peace, etc., but we have to trust the compiler's judgment.

Even reputable providers of secondary statistics have a bad habit. They state statistics to an impossible accuracy, sometimes three decimal digits. Your yardstick has 576 marks for 1/16th of an inch. If "democracy" could be measured with a yardstick, could it really be measured to 1/16th-inch precision? Even if it could, would you choose one home over another for even another ½" of democracy? For a specific example, *The Economist* assigns democracy scores of 8.13, 8.13, 8.08, 8.08, and 8.07 to Estonia, Spain, Czechia, Portugal, and Greece on a 10-point scale—in other words, 8.10 +/- 0.03. It's just not plausible that something as subjectively defined as "democracy" can be measured within

0.3%. But *The Economist* goes on to give the five countries three different ranks. For this book, I divided *The Economist's* three categories, "full democracy," "flawed democracy," and "hybrid system" into two subcategories each and assigned letter grades A, A-, B, B-, C, and C-. I have assigned letter grades for many statistics. They are compact and familiar and minimize the impact of using data from different years, which was sometimes necessary. There are always compromises, like the line drawn between the students with the highest B and the lowest A. It's never a mistake to refer to original sources before moving to a new home! (There are no "plus" grades because Excel would sort them after "minus" grades. This will help you if you download the spreadsheets, as I highly recommend.)

The third sort of statistics is simple rankings. They may be subjective and slanted to an audience. *International Living* recently published its annual compilation, "The 20 Best Places to Retire in 2025." The rankings are realistic for retirees, but probably not for digital nomads or job seekers or parents. You might download another "20 Best" list of tax havens. A tax-haven "resident" may be required to spend as few as ten days annually in their "home," making the rankings worthless for escapees. I have not included any of these rankings. I don't want to prime you with my own opinions, and I don't want to prime you with the rankings, since it is hard to know what drives them.

It seems like a no-brainer, but what's a country? Taiwan is excluded from United Nations data. Statistics for the United Kingdom, Great Britain, and England are conflated according to availability. I dealt with several similar (but less impactful) cases as was practical. No offense is intended toward the Scots or others.

Finally, I've included the United States and selected US cities in the tables for comparison.

Table I: The Cavalcade of Nations

"A man's [sic] homeland is wherever he prospers."

— Aristophanes
Greek Playwright, 450–388 BCE

It's time! Here are brief explanations of the statistics in Table I. If you are interested in details of the sources and the methods I used for assigning letter grades, etc., they can be found in Appendix A.

GOVERNMENT: DEMOCRACY AND LIBERTIES

I assigned A and A- to "full democracies" in our source, B and B- to "flawed democracies," and C and C- to "hybrid systems." *Authoritarian systems* have been excluded. The security of civil liberties is derived from the same source.

LANGUAGE: OFFICIAL_LANG AND ENG_PROFICIENCY

An official language is the customary language of government business—the language(s) used in legislative bodies and legal codes. Some countries give other languages limited legal status. For space reasons, I've deleted unfamiliar languages and long lists.

The measure of English proficiency is based on a self-selecting population, which is never ideal, but the results are consistent with anecdotal evidence.

PRICES: PURCH_POWER

"A dollar goes a lot further there," we've all heard. This column measures how much a US dollar will buy in the local economy. The UN assesses the cost in local currency of a market basket of essential local goods. The cost can be converted to US dollars according to prevailing market exchange rates. The market basket follows local preferences: rice in Asia, bread in Europe. Why the dollar's purchasing power varies is explained in the appendix. Choosing to consume an *American* market basket is likely to be *more expensive* than in the US.

Letter grades have been assigned based on C for the US. Countries with high inflation were graded F.

DEMOGRAPHICS: POPN_1000S, URBAN_PCT, POP_SQ_MILE, POP_65_UP, EXPATS, AND EXPATS_M_TO_F

All populations are stated in thousands and are otherwise self-explanatory: the total population, the percentage of the population living in urban areas, the population aged 65 and above, the number of US expatriates living in the country, and the sex ratio among the expats.

CLIMATE: KG_TROPICAL, KG_ARID, KG_TEMPERATE, KG_CONTINENTAL

The Köppen-Geiger Classification System classifies the world's climate zones into five categories: A = tropical, B = arid, C = temperate, D = continental, and E = polar. These columns indicate whether Köppen-Geiger A, B, C, and D zones are present in *any cities* in the country—uninhabited snow-capped mountains are excluded. Köppen subdivided the zones into more than 20 subzones, which are given for individual cities in Table II.

WELLBEING: HUMAN_CAPITAL, LIFE_EXPECTANCY, INCOME_LEVEL, HUMAN_DEVEL, PHYSICIANS_ PER_1000

These statistics are based on World Bank and United Nations data sets. I chose them to represent the overall well-being of a country's citizens. The Human Capital Index estimates the education and good health a baby born in 2020 will have accumulated by age 18. Life expectancy is an estimate of the number of years a newborn will live.

The UN divides countries into very high, high, high-medium, low-medium, and low incomes. These are A, B, C, D, and F in the income level column (but in fact, all "F" countries have authoritarian regimes).

The Human Development Index is a UN index of general well-being in a country.

SAFETY: ROAD_DEATHS, MURDERS, GUNS_PER_100, AND GUNS_FOR_SELF_DEFENSE

These columns report on safety and security concerns: annual road and traffic death rates per 100,000 residents, murders per 100,000 residents, the rate of gun ownership, and the permissibility of gun ownership for personal defense.

I report permissibility according to Wikipedia as described in the appendix.

- ‣ Y = Yes. There are no or very permissive regulations. Law enforcement authorities *shall* issue permits without discretion.
- ‣ M = Maybe. Law enforcement authorities exercise discretion and *may* issue permits.
- ‣ P = Partial. There are substantial non-discretionary grounds for denying permits.
- ‣ N = No. Gun permits are not issued on self-defense grounds.

THE TRUMPSTER FIRE ESCAPE ALMANAC

COUNTRY	CAPITAL	DEMOCRACY	LIBERTIES	OFFICIAL_LANG	ENG_PROFICIENCY	PURCH_POWER	PORN_1000S	URBAN_PCT	POP_SQ_MILE
Albania	Tirana	B-	B	Albanian	C	B	2476	65	263
Angola	Luanda	C-	D	Portuguese	F	F	36750	69	74
Argentina	Buenos Aires	B-	A-	Spanish	B	F	45538	92	43
Armenia	Yerevan	C	C	Armenian	C	A	2991	64	270
Australia	Canberra	A-	A	English	O	C	26659	87	9
Austria	Vienna	A-	A-	German	A	C	9132	60	284
Bangladesh	Dhaka	C-	D	Bengali	C	A	171467	40	3370
Belgium	Brussels	B	A-	Dutch/ French	B	C	11787	98	992
Benin	Porto Novo	C-	C-	French	F	A	14111	50	316
Bhutan	Thimphu	C	C-	Dzongkha		A	786	44	53
Bolivia	La Paz	C-	C	Spanish	C	A	12244	71	29
Bosnia and Herzegovina	Sarajevo	C	C	Bosnian		A	3185	50	162
Botswana	Gaborone	B	A-	English	O	A	2480	73	11
Brazil	Brasilia	B-	B-	Portuguese	D	A	211141	88	65
Bulgaria	Sofia	B-	B	Bulgarian/ English	B	A	6447	77	158
Canada	Ottawa	A-	A-	French	O	C	40098	82	11
Chile	Santiago	B	A	Spanish	C	B	19659	88	68
Colombia	Bogota	B-	B	Spanish	D	A	52321	82	121
Costa Rica	San Jose	A-	A	Spanish	C	B	5106	83	258
Croatia	Zagreb	B-	B-	Croatian/ Greek	A	B	3860	59	178
Cyprus	Nicosia	B	A-	Turkish	B	B	1345	67	373
Denmark	Copenhagen	A	A	Danish	A	D	5947	88	382
Dominican Republic	Santo Domingo	B-	B	Spanish	C	A	11331	84	604
Ecuador	Quito	C	C	Spanish	D	A	17980	65	186
El Salvador	San Salvador	C-	C	Spanish	C	A	6310	75	785
Estonia	Tallinn	A-	A-	Estonian	B	B	1370	70	82
Fiji	Suva	C	C	Fijian Fiji Hindi		A	924	59	130
Finland	Helsinki	A	A	Finnish/ Swedish	B	C	5584	86	47
France	Paris	A-	A-	French	C	C	68287	82	322

THE STATISTICS

POP_65_UP	EXPATS	EXPATS_M_F	KG_TROPICAL	KG_ARID	KG_TEMPERATE	KG_CONTINENTAL	LIFE_EXPECTANCY	HUMAN_CAPL	INCOME_LEVEL	HUMAN_DEVEL	PHYS_1000	ROAD_DEATHS	MURDERS	GUNS_PER_100	GUNS_SELF_DEF
448	2	0.6	-	-	C	-	77	C-	B	B	2	12	2	12	P
1033	0		A	B	C		62	F	C	C	0	26	4	11	p
5557	5	0.8	-	B	C	-	76	C-	B	A	4	14	5	7	Y
395	0			B	C	D	73	C-	B	B	3	20	2	6	Y
4634	117	1	A	-	C	-	83	A-	A	A	4	5	1	14	N
1841	12	1	-	-	C	D	81	B-	A	A	6	5	1	30	P
10838	45	2.2	A	-	C	-	74	D-	C	C	1	15	2	0	P
2375	16	1		-	C	-	82	A-	A	A	3	6	1	13	P
436	0		A				60	F	C	D	0	27	1	0	P
50	0						72	D-	C	C	1	16	2	1	-
680	5	0.9	A	B	C	-	65		C	C	1	21	4	2	P
689	0						75	C-	B	B	2	14	1	31	M
98	1	1.1	-	B	-	-	66	F	B	B	0	26	10	4	P
22452	22	1.1	A	B	C	-	73	C-	B	B	2	16	22	8	P
1407	3	0.8	-	-	C	D	74	C-	A	B	5	9	1	8	M
7762	273	1.2	A	-	C	D	81	A-	A	A	2	5	2	35	P
2692	17	1	-	B	C	-	80	B-	A	A	3	15	4	12	Y
4905	21	0.8	A	B	C	-	74	C-	B	B	2	15	28	10	M
598	0		A		C		77	C-	B	A	3	15	11	10	Y
881	2	1.1	-	-	C	-	78	B-	A	A	4	8	1	14	P
193	3	1.1	-	B	C	-	82	A-	A	A	4	6	1	34	M
1225	15	1	-	-	C	-	81	A-	A	A	4	4	1	10	N
859	15	0.9	A	-	-	-	74	D-	B	B	2	65	10	7	M
1455	28	0.7	A	B	C	-	78	C-	B	B	2	20	14	2	Y
505	5	1	A	-	-	-	71	D-	B	C	2	21	18	12	Y
287	1	0.6	-	-	-	D	78	A-	A	A	3	4	2	5	Y
59	0		A				68	D-	B	B	0	14	2	0	N
1317	5	0.7	-	-	-	D	81	A-	A	A	4	4	2	32	N
14852	62	1.5	-	-	C	-	82	A-	A	A	3	5	1	20	P

COUNTRY	CAPITAL	DEMOCRACY	LIBERTIES	OFFICIAL_LANG	ENG_PROFICIENCY	PURCH_POWER	PORN_1000S	URBAN_PCT	POP_SQ_MILE
Georgia	Tbilisi	C-	C	Georgian	C	A	3715	61	168
Germany	Berlin	A-	A	German	B	C	83280	78	621
Ghana	Accra	B-	C	English	O	F	33788	59	377
Greece	Athens	A-	A-	Greek	A	B	10406	81	210
Guatemala	Guatemala City	C-	C	Spanish	C	A	18125	53	431
Guyana	Georgetown	B-	B-	English	O	A	826	27	11
Honduras	Tegucigalpa	C	C	Spanish	C	A	10645	60	242
Hungary	Budapest	B-	B-	Hungarian	B	B	9592	73	274
Iceland	Reykjavik	A	A	Icelandic		D	393	94	10
India	New Delhi	B	B-	Hindi/English	O	A	1438070	36	1242
Indonesia	Jakarta	B-	C	Indonesian	D	A	281190	59	382
Ireland	Dublin	A	A	Irish/English	O	D	5308	64	194
Ishrael	Jerusalem	B	C	Hebrew	C	C	9757	93	
Italy	Rome	B	B	Italian	C	B	58993	72	517
Jamaica	Kingston	B-	A-	English	O	B	2840	57	679
Japan	Tokyo	A-	A	Japanese	D	B	124517	92	889
Kenya	Nairobi	C	C-	Swahili	B	A	55339	30	247
Latvia	Riga	B	A-	Latvian		B	1877	69	78
Lesotho	Maseru	B-	B-	Sesotho		A	2311	30	195
Liberia	Monrovia	C	C	English	O	A	5493	54	144
Lithuania	Vilnius	B	A-	Lithuanian	B	B	2872	69	117
Luxembourg	Luxembourg	A-	A	Luxembourgish/ French	B	C	666	92	657
Madagascar	Antananarivo	C	C-	Malagasy	D	A	31196	41	135
Malawi	Lilongwe	C	B-	English	F	F	21104	18	565
Malasia	Kuala Lumpur	B	C	Malay	B	A	35126	79	274
Malta	Valletta	B	A-	Maltese/ English		B	553	95	4302
Mauritius	Port Louis	A-	A-	English/ French	O	A	1261	61	1637
Mexico	Mexico City	C	C	Spanish	D	B	129740	82	171
Moldova	Chisinau	B-	B-	Romanian	C	A	2458	43	228
Mongolia	Ulaanbaatar	B-	C	Mongolian	D	A	3481	69	6
Montenegro	Podgorica	B-	B	Montenegrin		A	616	69	119
Morocco	Rabat	C	C-	Arabic/Berber	D	A	37713	65	217

POP_65_UP	EXPATS	EXPATS_M_F	KG_TROPICAL	KG_ARID	KG_TEMPERATE	KG_CONTINENTAL	LIFE_EXPECTANCY	HUMAN_CAPL	INCOME_LEVEL	HUMAN_DEVEL	PHYS_1000	ROAD_DEATHS	MURDERS	GUNS_PER_100	GUNS_SELF_DEF
569	0	0.6	-	-	C	D	72	C-	B	A	6	12	2	10	Y
18980	153	0.8	-	-	C	D	81	A-	A	A	5	4	1	20	P
1227	1	1.1	A	B	-	-	64	D-	C	C	0	26	2	8	Y
2444	23	1.2	-	B	C	-	81	B-	A	A	6	8	1	18	P
858	9	0.8	A	-	C	-	69	D-	B	C	1	23	20	12	M
54	1	0.8	A	-	-	-	66	D-	A	B	1	22	16	16	M
457	7	0.8	A	-	-	-	71	D-	C	C	0	16	38	14	Y
1997	9	0.9	-	-	C	D	76	B-	A	A	3	8	1	10	P
60	0						82	B-	A	A	5	2	0	32	N
99541	33	1	A	B	C	-	68	D-	C	C	1	16	3	5	M
19820	13	0.7	A	-	-	-	68	D-	B	B	1	11		0	P
825	35	1.3	-	-	C	-	83	A-	A	A	4	3	0	7	P
1211	77	1.1	-	B	C	-	83	B-	A	A	4	4	2	7	M
14288	54	1.3	A	-	C	-	83	B-	A	A	4	5	0	14	Y
223	6	0.9	A	-	-	-	71	D-	B	B	1	15	52	9	M
36809	58	1.2	A	-	C	D	84	A-	A	A	3	4	0	0	N
1612	0		A	B	C		62	D-	C	C	0	28	5	2	M
400	1	0.6	-	-	C	D	75	B-	A	A	3	8	3	10	Y
88	0	0.9	-	-	C	-	53	F	C	D	0	32		5	M
180	0	0.9	A	-	-	-	61	F	D	D	0	39		2	N
570	1	1	-	-	C	D	76	B-	A	A	5	8	3	14	Y
101	0				C		83	B-	A	A	3	4	1	19	N
1040	0		A	B	C		65	F	D	D	0	29		1	M
547	0		A		C		63	F	D	D	0	33		0	M
2617	0		A		C		76	C-	B	A	2	22	1	1	P
109	0						83	B-	A	A	4	4	0	28	N
163	0	1	A	-	-	-	74	C-	B	B	1	12	3	8	M
10362	799	1	A	B	C	-	75	C-	B	B	3	13	28	13	Y
384	0						69	C-	B	B	3	7	3	3	Y
169	0			B		D	73	C-	B	B	4	21	6	8	M
108	0	3.5	-	-	C	D	76	C-	B	A	3	8	2	39	M
3951	2	0.9	-	B	C	-	75	D-	C	C	1	17	2	5	P

COUNTRY	CAPITAL	DEMOCRACY	LIBERTIES	OFFICIAL_LANG	ENG_PROFICIENCY	PURCH_POWER	PORN_1000S	URBAN_PCT	POP_SQ_MILE
Namibia	Windhoek	B-	B	English	O	A	2963	55	9
Nepal	Kathmandu	C-	C	Nepali	C	A	29695	22	537
Netherlands	Amsterdam	A	A	Dutch	A	C	17877	93	1362
New Zealand	Wellington	A	A	English/Māori	O	C	5223	87	50
Nigeria	Abuja	C-	C-	English	B	F	227883	54	635
N Macedonia		B-	B	Macedonian	O	A	1828	59	188
Norway	Oslo	A	A	Norwegian	A	C	5520	84	39
Panama	Panama City	B-	B	Spanish	D	B	4459	70	154
Papua New Guinea	Port Moresby	B-	B	Hiri Motu/ Tok Pisin		B	10390	14	58
Paraguay	Asuncion	C	B	Spanish/ Guarani	C	A	6844	63	44
Peru	Lima	C	B-	Spanish	C	B	33846	79	68
Philippines	Manila	B-	B	Filipino/ English	B	A	114891	48	990
Poland	Warsaw	B	B	Polish	B	B	36687	60	312
Portugal	Lisbon	A-	A-	Portuguese	A	B	10578	68	295
Romania	Bucharest	B-	B	Romanina	B	A	19059	55	214
Senegal	Dakar	C	B-	French	F	A	18078	50	237
Serbia	Belgrade	B-	B	Serbian	B	A	6623	57	205
Sierra Leone	Freetown	C-	C	English	O	F	8461	44	297
Singapore	Singapore	B-	B-	English/Malay	A	C	5918	100	20334
Slovenia	Ljubljana	B	A-	Slovene		B	2120	56	272
South Africa	Pretoria Bloemfontein Cape Town	B	B	English Afrikaans	B	A	63212	69	133
Spain	Madrid	A-	A-	Spanish	C	B	48348	82	248
Sri Lanka	Colombo	B-	B-	Sinhala/Tamil	D	A	22037	19	929
Suriname	Paramaribo	B-	B	Dutch	B	F	629	66	10
Sweden	Stockholm	A	A	Swedish	A	C	10537	89	67
Switzerland	Bern	A	A	German/ French/Italian	B	D	8888	74	575
Tanzania	Dodoma	C	C-	Swahili/ English	D	A	66618	37	189
Thailand	Bangkok	B-	C	Thai	F	A	71702	54	364

POP_65_UP	EXPATS	EXPATS_M_F	KG_TROPICAL	KG_ARID	KG_TEMPERATE	KG_CONTINENTAL	LIFE_EXPECTANCY	HUMAN_CAPL	INCOME_LEVEL	HUMAN_DEVEL	PHYS_1000	ROAD_DEATHS	MURDERS	GUNS_PER_100	GUNS_SELF_DEF
106	1	1.4	-	B	-	-	58	F	B	C	1	35	12	15	M
1889	0				C		70	D-	C	C	1	16	2	2	M
3603	35	1.1	-	-	C	-	82	A-	A	A	4	4	1	3	N
877	36	1.1	-	-	C	D	83	A-	A	A	4	10	3	26	N
6901	0		A	B			54	F	C	D	0	21	22	3	N
320	0						74	C-	B	B	3	5	1	30	P
1023	19	1	-	-	C	D	83	A-	A	A	5	2	0	29	P
404	17	0.6	A	-	C	-	77	D-	A	A	2	14	13	11	Y
348	1	0.2	A	-	-	-	66	F	C	C	0	13		1	N
436	2	0.9	A	-	C	-	70	D-	B	B	4	22	8	17	Y
3044	41	0.5	A	B	C	-	73	C-	B	B	2	14	6	2	P
6046	38	0.9	A	B	-	-	72	D-	C	B	1	12	4	4	M
7176	18	0.8	-	-	C	D	77	A-	A	A	3	9	1	2	P
2551	8	1.1	-	-	C	-	82	A-	A	A	6	8	1	21	P
3765	6	0.9	-	B	C	D	75	C-	A	A	3	10	1	3	P
649	1	1	A	B	-	-	68	F	C	D	0	24		2	M
1480	1	1	-	-	C	D	75	B-	B	A	3	8	1	39	P
271	0	0.6	A	-	-	-	60	F	D	D	0	33	2	0	M
775	0						83	A	A	A	3	2	0	0	P
452	1	0.8	-	-	C	D	81	A-	A	A	3	5	0	16	P
4118	7	0.9	-	B	C	-	61	F	B	B	1	22	42	10	M
9986	57	1.1	A	B	C	-	83	B-	A	A	4	4	1	8	P
2587	1	1	A	-	-	-	77	C-	C	B	1	20	3	2	P
48	0		A				70		B	C	1	15	6	16	M
2164	23	0.9	-	-	C	D	83	A-	A	A	4	3	1	23	P
1743	39	1.1	-	-	C	D	83	A-	A	A	4	2	0	28	
2027	1	1	A	-	C	-	67	F	C	D	0	31	4	1	M
10553	4	0.4	A	-	-	-	80	C-	B	A	1	32		15	M

COUNTRY	CAPITAL	DEMOCRACY	LIBERTIES	OFFICIAL_LANG	ENG_PROFICIENCY	PURCH_POWER	PORN_1000S	URBAN_PCT	POP_SQ_MILE
Timor-Leste		B	B	Portuguese/ Tetum		A	1384	32	238
Trinidad and Tobago	Port of Spain	B	B	English	O	B	1368	53	690
Tunisia	Tunis	C-	C	Arabic	D	A	12200	71	202
Uganda	Kampala	C-	C-	English	C	A	48657	27	611
Ukraine	Kyiv	C-	C-	Ukrainian	C	A	37733	70	183
United Kingdom	London	A-	A	English	O	C	68350	85	726
United States	Washington	B	A-	English	O	C	334915	83	94
Uruguay	Montevideo	A-	A	Spanish	C	B	3388	96	50
Zambia	Lusaka	C	C	English	O	A	20724	46	70

THE STATISTICS

POP_65_UP	EXPATS	EXPATS_M_F	KG_TROPICAL	KG_ARID	KG_TEMPERATE	KG_CONTINENTAL	LIFE_EXPECTANCY	HUMAN_CAPL	INCOME_LEVEL	HUMAN_DEVEL	PHYS_1000	ROAD_DEATHS	MURDERS	GUNS_PER_100	GUNS_SELF_DEF
74	0						69	D-	C	C	1	12		0	N
162	0		A				75	C-	A	A	3	9	29	3	M
1118	1	0.9	-	B	C	-	74	D-	C	B	1	16	5	1	N
1046	1	1.1	A	-	C	-	64	F	D	C	0	29	8	1	P
7002	3	0.8	-	B	C	D	69	C-	B	B	0	10	4	10	N
13149	171	1.3	-	-	C	D	82	A-	A	A	3	3	1		
58382	0			B	C	D	77	B-	A	A	4	13	7	120	P
536	1	0.9	-	-	C	-	78	C-	A	A	5	15	9	35	Y
394	1	0.8	A	B	C	-	62	F	C	C	0	20		1	M

35

Table II: The Cities

"A great city is that which has the greatest men and women."

— Walt Whitman
American Poet, 1819–1892

Table II has a row for each of 467 cities. The cities were chosen according to size and climate zones. In each country, the two largest cities were chosen for each Köppen-Geiger zone. Angola has five zones and is represented by nine cities (since one zone only had one city). Belgium has one zone and two cities.

POPULATION: POPN

This column gives the number of inhabitants of the city in thousands.

Source:

- "Geonames—all cities with a population >1,000." Opendatasoft, https://public.opendatasoft.com/explore/dataset/ geonames-all-cities-with-a-population-1000/ export/?flg=en-us&disjunctive.cou_name_ en&sort=name

CLIMATE CATEGORY: KG

The Köppen-Geiger Climate Classification divides the world's climates into five major categories (A–E) and more than 20 subcategories. Each subcategory is defined by specific numeric standards for things like coldest month, seasonality of rainfalls, and the like.

Climate zones A–E can be described in layman's terms as follows:

- A comprises tropical climates, with high average temperatures throughout the year and lots of rain.
- B consists of desert and semi-arid climates. They have low rainfall and at least one warm month.
- C encompasses temperate climates. Temperate climates have at least one cold month and one warm month.
- D's continental climates have at least one month averaging below freezing and another above 50 degrees F.
- E is made up of polar and alpine climates with no warm months.

These are subdivided further:

- Af = Tropical rainforest climate
- Am = Tropical monsoon climate
- Aw and As = Wet and dry savanna climates
- BWh, BWk = Hot and cold desert climates
- BSh, BSk = Hot and cold semi-arid climates
- Cfa = Humid subtropical climate
- Cfb = Temperate oceanic climate or subtropical highland climate
- Cfc = Subpolar oceanic climate
- Cwa = Monsoon-influenced humid subtropical climate

- Cwb = Subtropical highland climate
- Cwc = Cold subtropical highland climate
- Csa, Csb, Csc = Hot-, warm- and cold-summer Mediterranean climates
- Dfa, Dfb = Hot- and warm-summer humid continental climates
- Dfc = Subarctic climate
- Dfd = Extremely cold subarctic climate
- Dwa, Dwb = Monsoon-influenced hot-summer humid continental climate
- Dwb = Monsoon-influenced warm-summer humid continental climate
- Dwc = Monsoon-influenced subarctic climate
- Dwd = Monsoon-influenced extremely cold subarctic climate
- Dsa = Mediterranean-influenced hot-summer humid continental climate;
- Dsb = Mediterranean-influenced warm-summer humid continental climate
- Dsc = Mediterranean-influenced subarctic climate
- Dsd = Mediterranean-influenced extremely cold subarctic climate
- ET = Tundra climate; the warmest month really isn't warm.
- EF = Ice cap climate; eternal winter.

Despite the apparently large number, the Köppen classifications are still rather coarse. Most or all of Kansas, Missouri, Kentucky, Virginia, Oklahoma, Arkansas, Tennessee, North and South Carolina, Texas, Louisiana, Alabama, Mississippi, Maryland, Delaware, and New Jersey have a Cfa climate. However, California alone has several climate zones due to mountain ranges and oceans.

Sources:

- ‣ "Köppen Climate Classification." Wikipedia, https://en.wikipedia.org/wiki/Köppen_climate_ classification, accessed 4/25/2025.
- ‣ Koppen Climate Classification API. Aptitute Apps, LLC., https://rapidapi.com.
- ‣ "World Maps of Köppen-Geiger Climate Classification." University of Vienna, https://koeppen-geiger.vu-wien. ac.at/usa.htm, accessed 6 August 2025.

TEMPERATURES: MIN_TEMP, MAX_TEMP, AVG_TEMP

I derived these Fahrenheit temperatures from 2024's daily temperature readings on the Meteostat website. The **AVG_ TEMP** column shows the average of the year's 366 daily average temperatures. Although historical averages are available from other sources, it has been clear to residents of every country I've visited that temperatures have risen significantly over the past several years. In fact, the press reported recently that New York City's climate was recently reclassified as Cfa.

Even so, to mitigate the effects of the extreme outliers, I dropped the 14 hottest and 14 coldest days. Columns **MIN_ TEMP** and **MAX_TEMP** show the minimum and maximum of the remaining 352 days.

PRECIPITATION: PRECIP, PRECIP_DAYS, MAX_SNOW, SNOW_DAYS

PRCP displays the total precipitation for 2024 in inches, without excluding outliers.

PRCP_DAYS displays the number of days in 2024 with measurable precipitation.

MAX_SNOW reports the maximum depth of snow on the ground during 2024.

SNOW_DAYS shows the number of days when snow was on the ground.

DAYLIGHT: MAX_DAY_HRS

This column gives the length of the longest day and the longest night in hours. More precisely, it is the number of hours between sunrise and sunset. Daylight arrives before sunrise at dawn and remains after sunset until dusk. In polar regions, there is daylight in December without any sunrise at all. This number is easily computed from latitude.

GEOGRAPHIC COORDINATES: LATITUDE AND LONGITUDE

Latitude and longitude were required to search for climatic data, and I include them for completeness.

COUNTRY	CITY	POPN	KG_CLIMATE	MIN_TEMP	MAX_TEMP
Albania	Shkoder	88245	Cfb	33	100
Albania	Tirana	418495	Csa	32	99
Albania	Elbasan	100903	Csa	33	78
Albania	Pogradec	61530	Csb	27	68
Albania	Korce	58259	Csb	26	70
Angola	Lubango	600751	Aw	46	88
Angola	Cabinda	550000	Aw	68	91
Angola	Ondjiva	121537	BSh	46	100
Angola	Porto Amboim	91605	BSh	66	87
Angola	Benguela	555124	BWh	62	89
Angola	Lobito	357950	BWh	62	89
Angola	Luena	273675	Cwa	52	93
Angola	Huambo	595304	Cwb	50	87
Angola	Cuito	355423	Cwb	47	88
Argentina	Santiago del Estero	252192	BSh	30	104
Argentina	La Rioja	178872	BSh	32	105
Argentina	San Luis	169947	BSk	32	99
Argentina	Neuquen	231198	BWk	25	99
Argentina	Buenos Aires	2891082	Cfa	39	88
Argentina	Rosario	948312	Cfa	30	96
Argentina	Cordoba	1317298	Cwa	33	98
Argentina	San Miguel/Tucuman	548866	Cwa	38	100
Argentina	Salta	520683	Cwb	30	93
Armenia	Vagharshapat	46200	BSk	21	96
Armenia	Ararat	28832	BSk	23	75
Armenia	Alaverdi	13184	Cfa	19	84
Armenia	Kapan	33160	Cfb	25	85
Armenia	Stepanavan	23782	Cfb	14	77
Armenia	Yerevan	1093485	Dfb	21	78
Armenia	Gyumri	148381	Dfb	6	86
Australia	Townsville	180820	Aw	52	92
Australia	Sydney	5231147	Cfa	45	89
Australia	Gold Coast	640778	Cfa	50	87
Australia	Melbourne	4917750	Cfb	38	94
Australia	Canberra	367752	Cfb	24	90
Australia	Perth	2192229	Csa	42	100

THE STATISTICS

AVG_TEMP	PRECIP	PRECIP_DAYS	MAX_SNOW	SNOW_DAYS	MAX_DAY_HRS	LATITUDE	LONGITUDE
62	72.3	139	0	0	15.1	42.07	19.51
64	45.6	152	0	0	15	41.33	19.82
64	45.6	152	0	0	15	41.11	20.08
55	26.2	130	0	0	14.9	40.9	20.65
54	22.2	142	0	0	14.9	40.62	20.78
67	23.9	144	0	0	12.9	-14.92	13.49
79	57.8	297	0	0	12.3	-5.57	12.2
76	16.6	82	0	0	13	-17.07	15.73
77	35.3	155	0	0	12.6	-10.73	13.77
77	10.2	73	0	0	12.7	-12.58	13.41
77	11	89	0	0	12.7	-12.36	13.54
71	33.3	157	0	0	12.7	-11.78	19.92
68	55.1	170	0	0	12.8	-12.78	15.74
67	42.1	181	0	0	12.7	-12.38	16.93
71	27.1	121	0	0	13.8	-27.8	-64.26
69	24.2	84	2.8	3	13.9	-29.41	-66.85
65	33.5	105	0.4	2	14.2	-33.3	-66.34
60	9.4	72	0	0	14.7	-38.95	-68.06
64	51	116	1.6	17	14.3	-34.61	-58.38
64	43.5	139	0	0	14.2	-32.95	-60.64
66	44.5	131	0	0	14	-31.41	-64.18
68	77.4	156	0	0	13.7	-26.82	-65.22
64	52.4	178	0.8	3	13.5	-24.79	-65.41
57	20	124	0	0	14.9	40.17	44.29
57	17.6	120	0	0	14.8	39.83	44.71
49	152.7	140	0	0	15	41.1	44.67
56	38.8	180	0	0	14.8	39.21	46.41
45	82.5	117	0	0	15	41.01	44.39
49	20	124	0	0	14.9	40.18	44.51
46	26.2	163	0	0	14.9	40.79	43.85
77	54.5	123	0	0	13.2	-19.27	146.81
66	52.6	128	0	0	14.3	-33.87	151.21
69	61.2	180	0	0	13.8	-28	153.43
58	19.4	128	0	0	14.6	-37.81	144.96
56	21.1	110	0	0	14.4	-35.28	149.13
66	24.2	107	0	0	14.1	-31.95	115.86

COUNTRY	CITY	POPN	KG_CLIMATE	MIN_TEMP	MAX_TEMP
Australia	Mandurah	107641	Csa	49	97
Australia	Adelaide	1387290	Csb	39	92
Australia	Bunbury	76452	Csb	41	96
Austria	Vienna	1691468	Cfb	31	91
Austria	Linz	204846	Cfb	26	88
Austria	Graz	295424	Dfb	19	88
Austria	Salzburg	157245	Dfb	23	86
Austria	Dornbirn	49278	Dfc	24	84
Austria	Feldkirch	33420	Dfc	24	77
Bangladesh	Cox's Bazar	253788	Am	59	92
Bangladesh	Sylhet	237000	Am	55	95
Bangladesh	Khulna	1500689	Aw	57	99
Bangladesh	Rajshahi	763580	Aw	50	96
Bangladesh	Rangpur	1031388	Cwa	50	95
Bangladesh	Shibganj	378701	Cwa	51	93
Belgium	Brussels	1019022	Cfb	30	82
Belgium	Antwerpen	529247	Cfb	29	80
Benin	Parakou	255478	Aw	68	94
Benin	Abomey	117824	Aw	75	97
Bhutan	Thimphu	98676	ET	26	78
Bhutan	Paro	11448	ET	26	78
Bolivia	Riberalta	99070	Am	59	101
Bolivia	Trinidad	84259	Am	55	102
Bolivia	Villamontes	39800	Aw	41	107
Bolivia	Guayaramerin	36008	Aw	63	98
Bolivia	Oruro	208684	BSk	17	76
Bolivia	Sucre	224838	Cfb	38	77
Bolivia	Cochabamba	841276	Cfc	38	91
Bolivia	Sacaba	180726	Cfc	38	91
Bolivia	Tarija	159269	Cwa	30	96
Bolivia	Yacuiba	82803	Cwa	41	102
Bolivia	La Paz	2004652	Cwc	20	67
Bolivia	Viacha	86218	Cwc	20	67
Bosnia/Her	Bijeljina	37692	Cfa	26	97
Bosnia/Her	Trebinje	33178	Cfa	40	91
Bosnia/Her	Banja Luka	221106	Cfb	23	95

AVG_TEMP	PRECIP	PRECIP_DAYS	MAX_SNOW	SNOW_DAYS	MAX_DAY_HRS	LATITUDE	LONGITUDE
67	21.3	108	0	0	14.1	-32.53	115.72
62	11.4	100	0	0	14.4	-34.93	138.6
64	36.7	112	0	0	14.2	-33.33	115.64
57	33.7	137	0.8	9	15.9	48.21	16.37
54	42.5	270	2.4	18	15.9	48.31	14.29
52	38.4	130	0.4	1	15.7	47.07	15.45
53	60.8	208	4.7	21	15.8	47.8	13.04
52	85.8	246	5.9	18	15.8	47.41	9.74
50	0	0	0	0	15.7	47.23	9.6
79	150.6	142	0	0	13.3	21.44	92.01
77	222.5	173	0	0	13.5	24.9	91.87
80	0	0	0	0	13.4	22.81	89.56
77	72	169	0	0	13.5	24.37	88.6
77	71	131	0	0	13.6	25.75	89.25
77	74.2	163	0	0	13.6	25	89.32
53	41.7	215	0	0	16.3	50.85	4.35
53	40.9	237	0	0	16.4	51.22	4.4
81	41.6	64	0	0	12.5	9.34	2.63
81	32.2	64	0	0	12.4	7.18	1.99
57	85.4	306	0	0	13.7	27.47	89.64
57	85.4	306	0	0	13.7	27.43	89.41
82	85	201	0	0	12.6	-11.01	-66.05
82	112.6	211	0	0	12.9	-14.83	-64.9
77	50.2	159	0	0	13.3	-21.26	-63.47
80	47.8	210	0	0	12.6	-10.83	-65.36
54	20.7	149	1.6	5	13.1	-17.98	-67.15
57	29.8	191	0	0	13.1	-19.03	-65.26
66	30.3	150	0	0	13	-17.39	-66.16
66	30.3	150	0	0	13	-17.4	-66.04
66	40.1	159	0	0	13.3	-21.54	-64.73
75	49.3	149	0	0	13.3	-22.02	-63.68
47	45	198	0.4	2	13	-16.5	-68.15
47	45	198	0.4	2	13	-16.65	-68.3
58	24.3	138	0	0	15.4	44.76	19.21
64	54.5	153	0	0	15.1	42.71	18.34
56	34.3	167	11.8	14	15.4	44.78	17.19

COUNTRY	CITY	POPN	KG_CLIMATE	MIN_TEMP	MAX_TEMP
Bosnia/Her	Zenica	164423	Cfb	24	100
Bosnia/Her	Mostar	104518	Csa	34	104
Bosnia/Her	Bugojno	41378	Dfb	20	93
Bosnia/Her	Mrkonjic Grad	14737	Dfb	21	95
Bosnia/Her	Sarajevo	696731	Dfc	21	94
Bosnia/Her	Visoko	17890	Dfc	24	92
Botswana	Maun	85350	BSh	71	87
Brazil	Salvador	2711840	Af	70	90
Brazil	Rio de Janeiro	6747815	Am	64	93
Brazil	Manaus	2219580	Am	73	98
Brazil	Fortaleza	2400000	As	73	89
Brazil	Natal	896708	As	72	90
Brazil	Brasilia	2207718	Aw	52	91
Brazil	Goiania	1536097	Aw	56	99
Brazil	Campinas	1031554	Cfa	53	93
Brazil	Sao Paulo	12400232	Cfb	48	89
Brazil	Curitiba	1948626	Cfb	42	87
Brazil	Belo Horizonte	2721564	Cwa	55	91
Bulgaria	Plovdiv	346893	Cfa	26	98
Bulgaria	Ruse	143417	Cfa	24	100
Bulgaria	Sofia	1152556	Cfb	21	93
Bulgaria	Varna	312770	Cfb	26	93
Canada	Surrey	394976	Cfb	31	76
Canada	Burnaby	202799	Cfb	28	82
Canada	Hamilton	519949	Dfa	19	82
Canada	Windsor	278013	Dfa	15	86
Canada	Toronto	2600000	Dfb	13	85
Canada	Montreal	1762949	Dfb	10	84
Chile	Antofagasta	352638	BWk	50	76
Chile	Arica	185999	BWk	53	80
Chile	Puerto Montt	245902	Cfb	28	75
Chile	Osorno	135773	Cfb	30	82
Chile	Santiago	4837295	Csb	33	91
Chile	Puente Alto	568106	Csb	33	91
Colombia	Cali	2392877	Af	64	93
Colombia	Cucuta	777106	Af	69	98

THE STATISTICS

AVG_TEMP	PRECIP	PRECIP_DAYS	MAX_SNOW	SNOW_DAYS	MAX_DAY_HRS	LATITUDE	LONGITUDE
56	30.3	162	0	0	15.3	44.2	17.9
66	45.7	128	0.8	2	15.2	43.34	17.81
55	0	0	0	0	15.3	44.06	17.45
55	36.6	174	0	0	15.4	44.42	17.08
55	39.4	178	0	0	15.3	43.85	18.36
54	28.6	155	0	0	15.3	43.99	18.18
74	7.6	29	0	0	13.2	-19.98	23.42
79	49.4	279	0	0	12.8	-12.98	-38.49
76	36.2	166	0	0	13.4	-22.91	-43.18
82	67.4	251	0	0	12.2	-3.1	-60.02
82	56.2	222	0	0	12.2	-3.72	-38.54
80	47.5	319	0	0	12.3	-5.8	-35.21
72	41.4	162	0	0	12.9	-15.78	-47.93
76	43.4	166	0	0	13	-16.68	-49.25
73	44.7	157	0	0	13.4	-22.91	-47.06
68	48.9	183	0	0	13.5	-23.55	-46.64
66	60.1	208	0	0	13.6	-25.43	-49.27
73	36.7	147	0	0	13.2	-19.92	-43.94
59	19.6	123	0	0	15.1	42.15	24.75
58	21.9	117	0	0	15.3	43.85	25.95
54	18.9	113	4.7	22	15.1	42.7	23.32
57	19.4	105	0.4	2	15.2	43.22	27.92
51	65.8	210	9.4	9	16	49.11	-122.83
50	102.7	207	7.1	5	16	49.27	-122.95
51	33.9	163	0	0	15.2	43.25	-79.85
52	46.9	164	7.1	24	15.1	42.3	-83.02
51	37.2	155	12.6	59	15.3	43.71	-79.4
49	51.6	211	13.8	72	15.5	45.51	-73.59
62	0	1	0	0	13.5	-23.65	-70.4
66	0.7	14	0	0	13.1	-18.47	-70.3
49	33.4	179	0	0	15	-41.47	-72.94
51	48.1	192	0	0	14.9	-40.57	-73.13
60	22.7	53	0	0	14.2	-33.46	-70.65
60	22.7	53	0	0	14.2	-33.61	-70.58
75	101.3	321	0	0	12.2	3.44	-76.52
81	33.6	183	0	0	12.5	7.89	-72.51

COUNTRY	CITY	POPN	KG_CLIMATE	MIN_TEMP	MAX_TEMP
Colombia	Medellin	1999979	Am	55	89
Colombia	Bello	392939	Am	55	89
Colombia	Palmira	312519	As	64	93
Colombia	Barranquilla	1206319	Aw	72	95
Colombia	Monteria	490935	Aw	71	98
Colombia	Bogota	7674366	Cfb	39	73
Colombia	Soacha	313945	Cfb	39	73
Colombia	Pasto	392930	Csb	55	82
Costa Rica	Alajuela	47494	Af	62	91
Costa Rica	Mercedes Norte	26007	Af	60	86
Costa Rica	San Jose	335007	Am	60	86
Costa Rica	San Francisco	55923	Am	60	86
Costa Rica	Limon	63081	Cfb	68	90
Croatia	Rijeka	107964	Cfa	33	93
Croatia	Vinkovci	28111	Cfa	26	95
Croatia	Zagreb	663592	Cfb	29	94
Croatia	Osijek	75535	Cfb	25	96
Croatia	Split	149830	Csa	41	95
Croatia	Zadar	67309	Csa	38	92
Cyprus	Pergamos	15000	BSh	44	98
Cyprus	Nicosia	200452	Csa	42	87
Cyprus	Limassol	154000	Csa	47	93
Denmark	Arhus	285273	Cfb	24	76
Denmark	Odense	180863	Cfb	26	76
Dom Rep	Puerto Plata	146000	Af	66	95
Dom Rep	Concepcion/Vega	102426	Af	64	95
Dom Rep	Salvaleon/Higueey	123787	Am	66	91
Dom Rep	La Romana	208437	Aw	66	91
Dom Rep	San Cristobal	154040	Aw	66	91
Ecuador	Quevedo	213842	Am	69	95
Ecuador	Guayaquil	2723665	Aw	69	95
Ecuador	Portoviejo	321800	Aw	66	92
Ecuador	La Libertad	75881	BSh	68	87
Ecuador	Salinas	43862	BSh	68	87
Ecuador	Quito	2781641	Cfb	44	73
Ecuador	Riobamba	264048	Cfb	46	77

THE STATISTICS

AVG_TEMP	PRECIP	PRECIP_DAYS	MAX_SNOW	SNOW_DAYS	MAX_DAY_HRS	LATITUDE	LONGITUDE
69	102.9	334	0	0	12.4	6.25	-75.56
69	102.9	334	0	0	12.4	6.34	-75.56
75	101.3	321	0	0	12.2	3.54	-76.3
83	29.9	85	0	0	12.6	10.97	-74.78
82	91.1	282	0	0	12.5	8.75	-75.88
58	68.6	226	1.6	34	12.3	4.61	-74.08
58	68.6	226	1.6	34	12.3	4.58	-74.22
66	84.3	211	2.4	5	12.1	1.21	-77.28
73	116.5	258	0	0	12.6	10.02	-84.21
71	111	282	0	0	12.6	10.01	-84.13
71	0	0	0	0	12.6	9.93	-84.08
71	111	282	0	0	12.6	9.99	-84.13
81	112.7	294	0	0	12.6	9.99	-83.04
61	73.1	163	0	0	15.5	45.33	14.44
56	25.6	131	0	0	15.5	45.29	18.8
59	41.2	125	2	31	15.5	45.81	15.98
57	22.8	134	0	0	15.5	45.55	18.69
66	28	96	0	0	15.2	43.51	16.44
63	47.9	147	0	0	15.3	44.12	15.23
71	8.8	74	0	0	14.4	35.04	33.71
69	10	100	0	0	14.4	35.18	33.36
70	14.5	57	0	0	14.3	34.68	33.04
50	34	193	0	0	17.4	56.16	10.21
50	27.7	153	0	0	17.2	55.4	10.39
79	60.4	293	0	0	13.2	19.79	-70.69
78	39.5	253	0	0	13.2	19.22	-70.53
80	44.9	248	0	0	13.1	18.62	-68.71
80	44.9	248	0	0	13.1	18.43	-68.97
78	65.5	302	0	0	13.1	18.42	-70.1
78	127.8	223	0	0	12.1	-1.03	-79.46
80	36.2	138	0	0	12.1	-2.2	-79.89
77	44	209	0	0	12.1	-1.05	-80.45
76	8	60	0	0	12.1	-2.23	-80.91
76	8	60	0	0	12.1	-2.21	-80.95
56	103.7	280	0	0	12	-0.23	-78.52
57	27.7	259	0	0	12.1	-1.67	-78.65

COUNTRY	CITY	POPN	KG_CLIMATE	MIN_TEMP	MAX_TEMP
Ecuador	Ambato	387309	Cfc	44	72
Ecuador	Tulcan	86498	Csc	37	68
Ecuador	Cuenca	636996	ET	44	80
Ecuador	Latacunga	205624	ET	44	75
El Salvador	San Salvador	525990	Aw	62	92
El Salvador	Soyapango	329708	Aw	62	92
Estonia	Tallinn	394024	Dfb	10	78
Estonia	Tartu	91407	Dfb	9	81
Estonia	Elva	5616	Dfc	9	81
Estonia	Tapa	5168	Dfc	3	76
Fiji	Ba	14596	Am	64	91
Finland	Helsinki	658864	Dfb	2	76
Finland	Espoo	256760	Dfb	1	77
Finland	Tampere	244315	Dfc	-8	76
Finland	Jyvaeskylae	144477	Dfc	###	80
France	Paris	2138551	Cfb	31	85
France	Lyon	522969	Cfb	29	89
France	Nimes	148236	Csa	32	96
France	Aix-en-Provence	146821	Csa	33	94
France	Nice	342669	Csb	41	87
France	Montpellier	248252	Csb	33	91
Georgia	Tbilisi	1049498	Cfa	21	93
Georgia	Batumi	172100	Cfa	39	84
Georgia	Sokhumi	65439	Cfb	40	84
Georgia	Ts'khinvali	32180	Cfb	23	89
Georgia	Gori	45557	Dfb	23	89
Georgia	Akhaltsikhe	16943	Dfb	19	65
Germany	Berlin	3426354	Cfb	30	84
Germany	Hamburg	1845229	Cfb	28	82
Ghana	Koforidua	151255	Am	69	99
Ghana	Kumasi	2544530	Aw	70	98
Ghana	Accra	1963264	Aw	73	95
Greece	Thessaloniki	317778	Csa	32	98
Greece	Patra	168034	Csa	37	98
Guatemala	Puerto Barrios	100593	Af	66	93
Guatemala	Quetzaltenango	180706	Am	33	82

THE STATISTICS

AVG_TEMP	PRECIP	PRECIP_DAYS	MAX_SNOW	SNOW_DAYS	MAX_DAY_HRS	LATITUDE	LONGITUDE
56	26.3	277	0	0	12.1	-1.25	-78.62
51	57.2	331	1.6	27	12	0.81	-77.72
59	65.4	307	0	0	12.2	-2.9	-79
57	86.3	321	0	0	12.1	-0.94	-78.62
80	75	204	0	0	12.8	13.69	-89.19
80	75	204	0	0	12.8	13.71	-89.14
46	19	127	11.4	68	18.3	59.44	24.75
46	23.1	178	10.6	74	18	58.38	26.73
46	23.1	178	10.6	74	17.9	58.22	26.42
44	20.1	128	0	0	18.2	59.26	25.96
78	90.9	188	0	0	13.1	-17.53	177.67
46	26.6	155	18.5	132	18.6	60.17	24.94
45	27.6	145	18.5	132	18.6	60.21	24.65
43	25	141	0	0	19.1	61.5	23.79
40	23.9	170	26	174	19.4	62.24	25.72
55	37.7	223	0.4	5	16	48.85	2.35
56	42.5	164	0.4	2	15.5	45.75	4.85
60	30.9	124	0	0	15.3	43.84	4.36
61	21.9	92	0.4	2	15.2	43.53	5.45
63	40.9	96	0	0	15.3	43.7	7.27
61	23.6	102	0	0	15.3	43.61	3.88
50	29.9	164	0	0	15	41.69	44.83
61	97.9	184	0	0	15	41.64	41.63
61	0	0	0	0	15.2	43.01	40.99
54	28.8	145	5.5	92	15.1	42.23	43.97
54	28.8	145	5.5	92	15.1	41.98	44.12
50	31	176	0	0	15	41.64	42.98
53	21.8	155	1.6	7	16.6	52.52	13.41
52	39.9	209	2.8	11	16.8	53.55	9.99
82	42.7	221	0	0	12.4	6.09	-0.26
82	42.3	228	0	0	12.4	6.69	-1.62
82	43.4	234	0	0	12.3	5.56	-0.2
63	21.1	92	0	0	14.9	40.64	22.93
65	30.1	125	0	0	14.7	38.24	21.73
80	118.1	286	0	0	12.9	15.73	-88.59
58	95.6	312	0	0	12.9	14.83	-91.52

COUNTRY	CITY	POPN	KG_CLIMATE	MIN_TEMP	MAX_TEMP
Guatemala	Villa Canales	155423	Am	53	91
Guatemala	Guatemala City	994938	Aw	53	91
Guatemala	Villa Nueva	618397	Aw	53	91
Guatemala	Coban	212047	Cfb	50	82
Guatemala	Huehuetenango	79426	Cfb	41	91
Guatemala	Totonicapan	103952	Cwb	33	82
Guyana	Georgetown	235017	Af	74	92
Guyana	Skeldon	5859	Af	73	92
Guyana	New Amsterdam	35039	As	74	91
Guyana	Rosignol	5782	As	74	91
Honduras	La Ceiba	222055	Af	65	92
Honduras	Choloma	139100	Af	65	102
Honduras	El Progreso	100810	Am	65	102
Honduras	La Lima	45955	Am	65	102
Honduras	Tegucigalpa	850848	Aw	55	92
Honduras	Ciudad Choluteca	75872	Aw	72	104
Hungary	Budapest	1741041	Cfb	28	91
Hungary	Debrecen	202402	Cfb	25	93
Iceland	Reykjavik	118918	ET	15	59
Iceland	Kopavogur	37959	ET	15	59
India	Navi Mumbai	2600000	Am	64	96
India	Coimbatore	2136916	Am	69	93
India	Indore	1837041	As	50	104
India	Tirunelveli	1435844	As	71	99
India	Chennai	4681087	Aw	70	100
India	Delhi	10927986	BSh	44	111
India	Bengaluru	8443675	BSh	60	98
India	Kanpur	2823249	Csa	43	92
India	Bhopal	1599914	Csa	51	91
India	Lucknow	2472011	Cwa	45	109
India	Patna	1599920	Cwa	49	107
Indonesia	Jakarta	8540121	Af	73	95
Indonesia	Bekasi	2564940	Af	78	92
Indonesia	Bandung	2444160	Am	60	87
Indonesia	Surabaya	2874314	Aw	75	97
Ireland	Dublin	1024027	Cfb	31	72

THE STATISTICS

AVG_TEMP	PRECIP	PRECIP_DAYS	MAX_SNOW	SNOW_DAYS	MAX_DAY_HRS	LATITUDE	LONGITUDE
69	62.9	222	0	0	12.9	14.48	-90.53
69	62.9	222	0	0	12.9	14.64	-90.51
69	62.9	222	0	0	12.9	14.53	-90.59
67	93.5	287	0	0	12.9	15.47	-90.37
64	42.7	198	0	0	12.9	15.32	-91.47
58	95.6	312	0	0	12.9	14.91	-91.36
84	69.9	263	0	0	12.4	6.8	-58.16
81	63.2	305	0	0	12.3	5.87	-57.15
81	68.8	313	0	0	12.4	6.25	-57.52
81	68.8	313	0	0	12.4	6.27	-57.54
79	143.9	165	0	0	12.9	15.76	-86.78
80	68.7	195	0	0	12.9	15.61	-87.95
80	68.7	195	0	0	12.9	15.4	-87.8
80	68.7	195	0	0	12.9	15.43	-87.92
73	56.1	204	0	0	12.8	14.08	-87.21
83	118.8	226	0	0	12.8	13.3	-87.19
56	19.7	147	0	0	15.8	47.5	19.04
55	13.8	110	0	0	15.8	47.53	21.62
40	52.5	231	0	0	20.5	64.14	-21.9
40	52.5	231	0	0	20.4	64.11	-21.91
83	126.8	137	0	0	13.1	19.04	73.02
81	39.2	153	0	0	12.6	11.01	76.97
77	31.6	121	0	0	13.4	22.72	75.83
83	42.2	244	0	0	12.5	8.73	77.68
83	56.3	208	0	0	12.8	13.09	80.28
77	461	84	0	0	13.8	28.65	77.23
75	47.9	152	0	0	12.8	12.97	77.59
77	48.6	104	0	0	13.7	26.47	80.35
77	69.6	118	0	0	13.4	23.25	77.4
77	41	100	0	0	13.7	26.84	80.92
81	36.4	113	0	0	13.6	25.59	85.14
84	93.2	299	0	0	12.4	-6.21	106.85
84	93.2	299	0	0	12.4	-6.23	106.99
73	92.8	292	0	0	12.4	-6.92	107.61
84	76.9	222	0	0	12.4	-7.25	112.75
50	27.3	234	0.4	1	16.8	53.33	-6.25

COUNTRY	CITY	POPN	KG_CLIMATE	MIN_TEMP	MAX_TEMP
Ireland	South Dublin	278749	Cfb	31	71
Israel	Beersheba	186600	BWh	45	87
Israel	Jerusalem	971800	Csa	41	95
Israel	West Jerusalem	400000	Csa	41	95
Italy	Milan	1371498	Cfa	28	91
Italy	Turin	847287	Cfa	28	89
Italy	Bologna	394843	Cfb	30	95
Italy	Trieste	204338	Cfb	36	92
Italy	Catania	311584	Csa	37	95
Italy	Messina	219948	Csa	49	93
Italy	Rome	2318895	Csb	33	98
Jamaica	New Kingston	583958	Af	68	94
Jamaica	Linstead	20660	Af	68	94
Jamaica	Montego Bay	82867	Am	71	94
Jamaica	Falmouth	7779	Am	71	94
Japan	Tokyo	8336599	Cfa	34	94
Japan	Osaka	2753862	Cfa	36	95
Kenya	Kakamega	1867579	Af	55	84
Kenya	Kisumu	397957	Af	61	87
Kenya	Karuri	194342	Aw	53	84
Kenya	Garissa	163399	BWh	71	102
Kenya	Mandera	114718	BWh	72	99
Kenya	Eldoret	475716	Cfb	51	80
Kenya	Kitale	162174	Cfb	53	86
Kenya	Nakuru	570674	Csb	53	87
Kenya	Nairobi	4397073	Cwb	53	84
Kenya	Ruiru	490120	Cwb	51	85
Latvia	Liepaja	85132	Cfb	21	80
Latvia	Ventspils	42644	Cfb	23	77
Latvia	Riga	742572	Dfb	19	79
Latvia	Daugavpils	111564	Dfb	12	53
Lesotho	Nako	13146	Cfb	30	87
Lesotho	Kolo	5233	Cfb	30	87
Lesotho	Maseru	359753	Cfb	30	87
Lesotho	Maputsoe	61916	Cwb	27	87
Liberia	Kakata	52247	Am	75	91

THE STATISTICS

AVG_TEMP	PRECIP	PRECIP_DAYS	MAX_SNOW	SNOW_DAYS	MAX_DAY_HRS	LATITUDE	LONGITUDE
50	36.4	258	0.4	1	16.7	53.29	-6.34
70	4	53	0.4	3	14	31.25	34.79
65	0	0	0	0	14.1	31.77	35.22
65	0	0	0	0	14.1	31.78	35.22
59	11.6	122	0	0	15.5	45.46	9.19
56	45.7	166	0.4	1	15.4	45.07	7.69
59	42.4	154	0	0	15.4	44.49	11.34
60	60.4	163	0	0	15.5	45.65	13.78
66	11.8	89	0	0	14.6	37.49	15.07
69	27.8	105	0	0	14.7	38.19	15.55
63	34.1	155	0	0	15.1	41.89	12.51
84	33.2	97	0	0	13.1	18.01	-76.78
84	33.2	97	0	0	13.1	18.14	-77.03
82	47.5	140	0	0	13.1	18.47	-77.92
82	47.5	140	0	0	13.1	18.49	-77.66
63	60.5	179	0	0	14.4	35.69	139.69
65	63	115	0	0	14.3	34.69	135.5
68	56.4	266	0	0	12	0.28	34.75
74	39.8	242	0	0	12	-0.1	34.76
65	33.7	238	0	0	12	-0.7	37.18
84	12.9	105	0	0	12	-0.45	39.65
86	13.8	88	0	0	12.2	3.94	41.86
63	36.3	258	0	0	12	0.52	35.27
67	61	215	0	0	12.1	1.02	35.01
66	42.3	236	0	0	12	-0.31	36.07
68	33.7	238	0	0	12.1	-1.28	36.82
67	40.2	228	0	0	12.1	-1.15	36.96
49	21.8	156	4.3	12	17.5	56.5	21.01
49	19.1	130	0	0	17.7	57.39	21.56
49	22.5	153	0	0	17.6	56.95	24.11
48	20.8	142	5.5	21	17.3	55.88	26.53
58	28.1	111	0	0	13.9	-29.62	27.77
58	28.1	111	0	0	13.9	-29.69	27.69
58	28.1	111	0	0	13.9	-29.32	27.48
59	29.5	143	0	0	13.8	-28.89	27.9
80	100.1	327	0	0	12.4	6.53	-10.35

COUNTRY	CITY	POPN	KG_CLIMATE	MIN_TEMP	MAX_TEMP
Liberia	Harbel	38208	Am	75	91
Lithuania	Klaipeda	172292	Cfb	23	81
Lithuania	Vilnius	542366	Dfb	18	83
Lithuania	Kaunas	289380	Dfb	18	81
Luxembourg	Luxembourg	76684	Cfb	24	82
Luxembourg	Esch-sur-Alzette	28228	Cfb	24	82
Madagascar	Toamasina	345107	Af	60	90
Madagascar	Antsiranana	136959	Aw	64	93
Madagascar	Toliara	178725	BSh	62	97
Madagascar	Fianarantsoa	203105	Cfb	49	87
Madagascar	Ambatondrazaka	50463	Cwa	53	87
Madagascar	Antananarivo	1349501	Cwb	46	89
Madagascar	Antsirabe	260907	Cwb	39	87
Malawi	Karonga	69486	Aw	59	93
Malawi	Mangochi	60338	Aw	60	93
Malawi	Lilongwe	1115815	Cwa	48	88
Malawi	Blantyre	902588	Cwa	52	88
Malawi	Dedza	34882	Cwb	46	81
Malawi	Mzimba	29432	Cwb	52	87
Malaysia	Malacca	579000	Af	74	93
Malaysia	Kuantan	548014	Af	73	95
Malaysia	Alor Setar	417800	Am	73	98
Malaysia	Kota Kinabalu	500421	Cfb	74	94
Mauritius	Curepipe	78618	Am	58	84
Mauritius	Triolet	24361	Am	58	84
Mexico	Merida	1201000	Aw	59	107
Mexico	Monterrey	1135512	BSh	42	102
Mexico	Culiacan	808416	BSh	49	104
Mexico	Leon/Aldama	1721199	BSk	49	84
Mexico	Santiago/Queretaro	1594212	BSk	42	96
Mexico	Mexicali	1032686	BWh	41	111
Mexico	Hermosillo	812229	BWh	42	111
Mexico	Ciudad Juarez	1501551	BWk	32	100
Mexico	Zapopan	1476491	Csa	43	98
Mexico	Guadalajara	1385629	Csa	43	98
Mexico	Mexico City	12294193	Cwb	42	89

THE STATISTICS

AVG_TEMP	PRECIP	PRECIP_DAYS	MAX_SNOW	SNOW_DAYS	MAX_DAY_HRS	LATITUDE	LONGITUDE
80	100.1	327	0	0	12.4	6.25	-10.36
50	27	165	5.5	27	17.3	55.71	21.14
48	22	144	7.5	27	17	54.69	25.28
49	19.3	136	8.3	26	17.1	54.9	23.91
51	42.8	191	2.4	6	16.1	49.61	6.13
51	42.8	191	2.4	6	16.1	49.5	5.98
76	116.1	285	0	0	13.1	-18.15	49.4
81	70	192	0	0	12.7	-12.32	49.29
80	13.7	67	0	0	13.4	-23.35	43.67
66	37.8	230	0	0	13.3	-21.45	47.09
69	37.9	162	0	0	13.1	-17.83	48.42
66	45.8	145	0	0	13.1	-18.91	47.54
65	55.4	172	0	0	13.2	-19.87	47.03
75	49	190	0	0	12.6	-9.93	33.93
77	23.2	154	0	0	12.9	-14.48	35.26
71	26.6	145	0	0	12.8	-13.97	33.79
68	27.5	179	0	0	12.9	-15.78	35.01
63	31	180	0	0	12.9	-14.38	34.33
68	26.7	143	0	0	12.7	-11.9	33.6
82	94.4	311	0	0	12.1	2.2	102.24
81	88.6	292	0	0	12.2	3.81	103.33
83	97.5	292	0	0	12.4	6.12	100.36
82	74	285	0	0	12.3	5.97	116.07
71	60.4	238	0	0	13.2	-20.32	57.53
71	60.4	238	0	0	13.2	-20.06	57.55
82	55.9	194	0	0	13.3	20.98	-89.62
74	23.6	139	0	0	13.6	25.68	-100.32
79	12.9	29	0	0	13.5	24.79	-107.39
69	25.7	104	0	0	13.3	21.13	-101.67
66	11.4	46	0	0	13.3	20.59	-100.39
75	1.3	18	0	0	14.1	32.63	-115.45
78	3.2	31	0	0	13.9	29.1	-110.98
68	2.6	42	0	0	14.1	31.72	-106.46
69	36.1	117	0	0	13.3	20.72	-103.38
69	36.1	117	0	0	13.3	20.67	-103.39
65	45.5	151	0	0	13.2	19.43	-99.13

COUNTRY	CITY	POPN	KG_CLIMATE	MIN_TEMP	MAX_TEMP
Mexico	Iztapalapa	1815786	Cwb	42	89
Mongolia	Bayanhongor	30931	BSk	-7	22
Mongolia	Ulaangom	30092	BSk	###	17
Mongolia	Khovd	29800	BWk	-7	11
Mongolia	Mandalgovi	12339	BWk	###	23
Mongolia	Suehbaatar	22741	Dwb	###	86
Mongolia	Dzuunharaa	18830	Dwb	###	13
Mongolia	Tsetserleg	21620	Dwc	-5	29
Mongolia	Bulgan	17348	Dwc	###	34
Montenegro	Niksic	58212	Cfb	28	96
Montenegro	Plav	3615	Cfb	23	91
Montenegro	Podgorica	236852	Csa	33	100
Montenegro	Bar	17727	Csa	42	94
Montenegro	Pljevlja	19489	Dfb	20	67
Montenegro	Danilovgrad	5208	Dfb	33	100
Montenegro	Rozaje	9121	Dfc	23	91
Morocco	Marrakesh	995871	BSh	44	108
Morocco	Safi	336883	BSh	48	86
Morocco	Fes	1191905	Csa	35	100
Morocco	Tangier	1035141	Csa	46	91
Namibia	Windhoek	386219	BSh	46	95
Namibia	Rundu	75180	BSh	44	100
Namibia	Omaruru	11547	BSk	38	100
Namibia	Keetmanshoop	23049	BWh	39	102
Namibia	Mariental	14789	BWh	43	108
Namibia	Walvis Bay	73598	BWk	42	96
Namibia	Swakopmund	53009	BWk	42	96
Nepal	Birganj	268273	Cwa	46	94
Nepal	Biratnagar	244750	Cwa	48	94
Nepal	Kathmandu	1442271	Cwb	39	92
Nepal	Patan	299283	Cwb	39	92
Netherlands	Amsterdam	741636	Cfb	32	79
Netherlands	Utrecht	361742	Cfb	30	82
New Zealand	Auckland	417910	Cfb	41	76
New Zealand	Wellington	381900	Cfb	41	75
Nigeria	Port Harcourt	2120000	Am	71	98

THE STATISTICS

AVG_TEMP	PRECIP	PRECIP_DAYS	MAX_SNOW	SNOW_DAYS	MAX_DAY_HRS	LATITUDE	LONGITUDE
65	45.5	151	0	0	13.2	19.36	-99.06
35	5.6	29	10.2	106	15.6	46.19	100.72
31	2.6	25	14.2	120	16.1	49.98	92.07
38	2	20	2.4	51	15.8	48.01	91.64
39	4.8	15	3.5	100	15.5	45.76	106.27
35	12.1	97	6.3	134	16.2	50.23	106.21
35	38	16	47	114	16	48.85	106.46
37	6.2	37	3.1	86	15.8	47.48	101.45
33	0.9	8	3.9	77	16	48.81	103.53
57	72.8	143	11.8	6	15.2	42.77	18.94
53	0	0	0	0	15.1	42.6	19.95
62	62.2	133	0	0	15.1	42.44	19.26
66	53.5	108	0	0	15.1	42.09	19.1
54	30.8	142	11.8	32	15.2	43.36	19.36
62	62.2	133	0	0	15.1	42.55	19.15
53	0	0	0	0	15.2	42.83	20.17
71	6.2	29	0	0	14.1	31.63	-8
66	9.1	52	0	0	14.1	32.3	-9.24
65	15.8	82	0	0	14.3	34.03	-5
66	29.4	93	0	0	14.4	35.77	-5.8
71	9.6	76	0	0	13.4	-22.56	17.08
76	14.5	79	0	0	13.1	-17.92	19.77
74	7.8	55	0	0	13.3	-21.42	15.95
72	3.3	39	0	0	13.7	-26.58	18.13
80	0	0	0	0	13.5	-24.63	17.96
62	0	2	0	0	13.4	-22.96	14.51
62	0	2	0	0	13.4	-22.68	14.53
74	59.7	141	0	0	13.7	27.02	84.88
75	79.3	162	0	0	13.7	26.46	87.27
66	70.2	152	0	0	13.8	27.7	85.32
66	70.2	152	0	0	13.8	27.68	85.31
53	42.9	224	0	0	16.6	52.37	4.89
53	41.9	218	0.4	3	16.5	52.09	5.12
58	41.3	229	0	0	14.5	-36.85	174.76
57	34.8	183	0	0	15	-41.29	174.78
81	71.6	266	0	0	12.3	4.78	7.01

THE TRUMPSTER FIRE ESCAPE ALMANAC

COUNTRY	CITY	POPN	KG_CLIMATE	MIN_TEMP	MAX_TEMP
Nigeria	Ibadan	3649000	Aw	69	100
Nigeria	Kaduna	1850000	Aw	60	101
Nigeria	Kano	4910000	BSh	50	107
Nigeria	Maiduguri	1110000	BSh	58	107
Norway	Bergen	285911	Cfb	23	77
Norway	Trondheim	212660	Cfb	12	75
Norway	Alesund	52626	Cfc	25	70
Norway	Oslo	580000	Dfb	13	77
Norway	Drammen	103007	Dfb	7	77
Norway	Hamar	29479	Dfc	1	77
Norway	Lillehammer	28425	Dfc	2	56
Norway	Tromso	64448	ET	16	72
Panama	San Miguelito	321501	Am	71	95
Panama	Juan Diaz	100636	Am	71	95
Panama	Santiago/Veraguas	45355	Aw	70	98
Panama	Changuinola	17997	Cfb	73	87
Papua NG	Mount Hagen	33623	Af	55	80
Papua NG	Madang	27419	Af	72	89
Paraguay	Pedro Juan Cab	75109	Am	44	95
Paraguay	Concepcion	48123	Aw	46	104
Paraguay	Asuncion	1482200	Cfa	42	104
Paraguay	Ciudad/Este	301815	Cfa	44	98
Peru	Iquitos	377609	Af	69	96
Peru	Pucallpa	326040	Am	68	96
Peru	Cajamarca	201329	BSk	39	77
Peru	Chiclayo	552508	BWh	59	89
Peru	Piura	484475	BWh	59	96
Peru	Arequipa	1008290	BWk	43	73
Peru	Tacna	286240	BWk	50	84
Peru	Juliaca	245675	Cwb	26	69
Peru	Ayacucho	140033	Cwb	44	80
Peru	Cusco	428450	ET	32	75
Peru	Huaraz	118836	ET	39	84
Philippines	Budta	1273715	Af	73	95
Philippines	Malingao	1121974	Af	73	95
Philippines	Quezon City	2761720	Am	70	97

THE STATISTICS

AVG_TEMP	PRECIP	PRECIP_DAYS	MAX_SNOW	SNOW_DAYS	MAX_DAY_HRS	LATITUDE	LONGITUDE
81	31.6	209	0	0	12.4	7.38	3.91
77	33.2	148	0	0	12.6	10.53	7.44
79	40.4	91	0	0	12.7	12	8.52
83	25.7	98	0	0	12.7	11.85	13.16
48	110.7	255	15	19	18.6	60.39	5.32
44	41.6	212	5.1	38	20	63.43	10.4
47	49	211	0	0	19.5	62.47	6.15
45	41.4	195	20.5	95	18.5	59.91	10.75
44	35.9	176	0	0	18.4	59.74	10.2
42	23.1	187	0	0	18.8	60.79	11.07
38	37	170	0	0	18.9	61.12	10.47
41	47.7	204	50	187		69.65	18.96
81	110.8	312	0	0	12.5	9.05	-79.47
81	110.8	312	0	0	12.5	9.04	-79.44
79	104.4	292	0	0	12.5	8.1	-80.98
78	108.8	331	0	0	12.6	9.43	-82.52
66	79.2	323	0	0	12.3	-5.86	144.23
79	121.1	336	0	0	12.3	-5.22	145.79
73	40.4	173	0	0	13.4	-22.55	-55.73
77	64.7	155	0	0	13.4	-23.4	-57.43
76	72.3	147	0	0	13.6	-25.29	-57.65
73	59.9	117	0	0	13.6	-25.51	-54.61
79	102	306	0	0	12.2	-3.75	-73.25
81	82.7	226	0	0	12.5	-8.38	-74.55
59	74.2	275	0	0	12.4	-7.16	-78.5
70	2.7	34	0	0	12.4	-6.77	-79.84
75	8.2	72	0	0	12.3	-5.19	-80.63
62	22.7	127	0	0	13	-16.4	-71.54
64	1.8	23	0	0	13.1	-18.01	-70.25
50	40.9	199	0	0	12.9	-15.5	-70.13
61	57.2	213	0	0	12.8	-13.16	-74.22
55	56.8	282	0	0	12.8	-13.52	-71.97
62	50.2	260	0	0	12.6	-9.53	-77.53
81	95.5	305	0	0	12.4	7.2	124.44
81	95.5	305	0	0	12.4	7.16	124.48
82	90.6	208	0	0	12.9	14.65	121.05

COUNTRY	CITY	POPN	KG_CLIMATE	MIN_TEMP	MAX_TEMP
Philippines	Paranaque City	689992	Am	73	98
Poland	Wroclaw	634893	Cfb	23	87
Poland	Poznan	570352	Cfb	26	86
Poland	Warsaw	1702139	Dfb	25	88
Poland	Lodz	768755	Dfb	24	86
Portugal	Setubal	117110	Csa	41	91
Portugal	Evora	55620	Csa	40	73
Portugal	Lisbon	517802	Csb	46	88
Portugal	Amadora	178858	Csb	44	91
Romania	Braila	213569	Bsk	26	96
Romania	Bucharest	1877155	Cfa	25	99
Romania	Craiova	305689	Cfa	24	99
Romania	Iasi	378954	Cfb	17	95
Romania	Timisoara	315053	Cfb	24	97
Romania	Cluj-Napoca	316748	Dfb	21	92
Romania	Brasov	253200	Dfb	14	80
Senegal	Ziguinchor	205294	As	62	107
Senegal	Kolda	81098	Aw	60	110
Senegal	Dakar	2646503	Bsh	66	94
Senegal	Pikine	874062	Bsh	66	94
Senegal	Saint-Louis	209752	Bwh	62	104
Senegal	Richard-Toll	57878	Bwh	63	109
Serbia	Belgrade	1273651	Cfa	29	98
Serbia	Nis	250000	Cfa	24	100
Serbia	Kragujevac	147473	Cfb	25	98
Serbia	Cacak	117072	Cfb	21	96
Serbia	Leskovac	94758	Dfb	23	100
Serbia	Vranje	56199	Dfb	22	96
Sierra Leone	Bo	174354	Am	71	99
Sierra Leone	Bumpe	16123	Am	71	99
Slovenia	Maribor	97019	Cfb	22	89
Slovenia	Kranj	37941	Cfb	18	89
Slovenia	Ljubljana	272220	Dfb	24	91
Slovenia	Novo Mesto	24183	Dfb	24	90
South Africa	Bloemfontein	556000	Bsk	24	95
South Africa	Port Elizabeth	1050078	Cfa	42	84

THE STATISTICS

AVG_TEMP	PRECIP	PRECIP_DAYS	MAX_SNOW	SNOW_DAYS	MAX_DAY_HRS	LATITUDE	LONGITUDE
84	85.3	199	0	0	12.9	14.48	121.02
53	26.2	154	3.9	9	16.3	51.1	17.03
52	21.3	173	2	13	16.6	52.41	16.93
53	22.3	155	3.9	13	16.5	52.23	21.01
51	23.1	182	0	0	16.5	51.77	19.47
63	18.5	107	0	0	14.7	38.52	-8.89
62	24.1	106	0	0	14.7	38.57	-7.9
64	18.3	101	0	0	14.7	38.72	-9.13
63	19.2	109	0	0	14.7	38.75	-9.23
57	15.6	91	0.8	7	15.5	45.27	27.97
58	19.8	127	4.7	19	15.4	44.43	26.11
57	14.3	94	2.4	10	15.3	44.32	23.8
54	25.3	120	10.2	32	15.7	47.17	27.6
56	26.5	114	1.2	15	15.5	45.75	21.23
53	19.9	132	2	15	15.7	46.77	23.6
46	38.7	196	0	0	15.5	45.65	25.61
81	61.5	105	0	0	12.7	12.57	-16.27
84	53.1	100	0	0	12.8	12.89	-14.94
78	17.2	65	0	0	12.9	14.69	-17.44
78	17.2	65	0	0	12.9	14.76	-17.39
79	4.3	34	0	0	13	16.02	-16.49
82	7.9	38	0	0	13	16.46	-15.7
60	33.3	113	6.7	26	15.4	44.8	20.47
57	21.7	111	6.7	10	15.2	43.32	21.9
57	24.5	144	0	0	15.3	44.02	20.92
56	22.4	131	0	0	15.3	43.89	20.35
56	24.5	132	0	0	15.2	43	21.95
55	33.9	154	0	0	15.1	42.55	21.9
79	100.2	253	0	0	12.5	7.96	-11.74
79	100.2	253	0	0	12.5	7.89	-11.91
54	35.3	152	0	0	15.6	46.55	15.65
51	56	193	0	0	15.6	46.24	14.36
54	61.2	141	9.8	19	15.6	46.05	14.51
55	37.3	160	0	0	15.5	45.8	15.17
61	36.9	133	0	0	13.9	-29.12	26.21
64	33.5	177	0	0	14.3	-33.96	25.61

COUNTRY	CITY	POPN	KG_CLIMATE	MIN_TEMP	MAX_TEMP
South Africa	Pietermaritzburg	750845	Cfb	40	92
South Africa	Uitenhage	291052	Cfb	42	84
South Africa	Johannesburg	5635127	Cwb	34	88
South Africa	Soweto	1695047	Cwb	34	88
Spain	Madrid	3255944	BSk	35	99
Spain	Zaragoza	675301	BSk	34	100
Spain	Bilbao	345821	Cfb	39	84
Spain	Gasteiz/Vitoria	249176	Cfb	30	89
Spain	Sevilla	684234	Csa	39	100
Spain	Malaga	578460	Csa	44	94
Spain	Palma	409661	Csb	42	91
Spain	Valladolid	299265	Csb	30	96
Sri Lanka	Anuradhapura	60943	As	71	95
Sri Lanka	Jaffna	169102	Aw	74	93
Sri Lanka	Point Pedro	89810	Aw	74	93
Suriname	Paramaribo	223757	Af	74	95
Suriname	Lelydorp	18223	Af	73	95
Sweden	Stockholm	1515017	Cfb	15	77
Sweden	Malmoe	351749	Cfb	25	78
Sweden	Uppsala	177074	Dfb	12	77
Sweden	OErebro	155989	Dfb	14	77
Sweden	Umea	130224	Dfc	-7	72
Switzerland	Zurich	341730	Cfb	26	85
Switzerland	Geneve	183981	Cfb	28	88
Switzerland	Sankt Gellen	70572	Dfc	24	77
Switzerland	Lugano	63000	Dfc	33	87
Thailand	Nakhon Si Tham	102152	Af	73	98
Thailand	Hat Yai	191696	Am	68	97
Thailand	Chanthaburi	99819	Am	71	96
Thailand	Bangkok	5104476	Aw	73	100
Thailand	Samut Parkan	388920	Aw	72	99
Trinidad/Tobago	Chaguanas	67433	Am	70	94
Trinidad/Tobago	Arima	35000	Am	70	94
Tunisia	Sfax	277278	BSh	45	96
Tunisia	Sousse	164123	BSh	46	96
Tunisia	Gabes	110075	BWh	41	104

THE STATISTICS

AVG_TEMP	PRECIP	PRECIP_DAYS	MAX_SNOW	SNOW_DAYS	MAX_DAY_HRS	LATITUDE	LONGITUDE
64	30.8	174	0	0	13.9	-29.62	30.39
64	33.5	177	0	0	14.2	-33.76	25.4
62	16.2	113	0	0	13.6	-26.2	28.04
62	16.2	113	0	0	13.6	-26.27	27.86
60	13.8	84	0	0	14.9	40.42	-3.7
61	14.3	91	0	0	15	41.66	-0.88
60	53.1	194	1.2	4	15.2	43.26	-2.93
54	34.5	173	0	0	15.2	42.85	-2.67
66	23	71	1.2	4	14.6	37.38	-5.97
66	20	63	0	0	14.5	36.72	-4.42
65	14.5	111	1.6	4	14.8	39.57	2.65
56	19.2	110	0.8	5	15	41.66	-4.72
81	57.2	261	0	0	12.5	8.31	80.41
83	48.7	236	0	0	12.6	9.67	80.01
83	48.7	236	0	0	12.6	9.82	80.23
81	60.3	295	0	0	12.3	5.87	-55.17
81	64.4	298	0	0	12.3	5.7	-55.23
47	17	113	7.1	33	18.3	59.33	18.07
50	22.4	151	0	0	17.2	55.61	13
45	18.4	119	0	0	18.4	59.86	17.64
45	22.6	140	0	0	18.2	59.27	15.21
40	27.6	136	0	0	20.3	63.83	20.26
51	50.4	195	11	23	15.7	47.37	8.55
54	35.7	162	5.9	7	15.6	46.2	6.15
50	0	0	0	0	15.8	47.42	9.37
55	70.3	134	2.8	2	15.6	46.01	8.96
82	136.1	291	0	0	12.5	8.43	99.97
82	126.2	275	0	0	12.4	7.01	100.48
83	139.1	260	0	0	12.7	12.61	102.1
85	105.9	219	0	0	12.8	13.75	100.5
85	76.9	206	0	0	12.8	13.6	100.6
81	54.8	179	0	0	12.8	10.52	-61.42
81	54.8	179	0	0	12.6	10.64	-61.28
70	6.4	60	0	0	14.3	34.74	10.76
69	10	87	0	0	14.4	35.83	10.64
71	6.6	59	0	0	14.3	33.88	10.1

COUNTRY	CITY	POPN	KG_CLIMATE	MIN_TEMP	MAX_TEMP
Tunisia	Gafsa	81232	BWh	37	105
Tunisia	Tunis	693210	Csa	45	102
Tunisia	Bizerte	115268	Csa	44	87
Uganda	Kampala	1353189	Af	62	85
Uganda	Jinja	93061	Af	62	85
Uganda	Entebbe	62969	Am	64	84
Uganda	Busia	43200	Am	61	90
Uganda	Gulu	146858	Aw	63	96
Uganda	Lira	119323	Aw	63	95
Uganda	Kabale	43500	Cfb	55	79
Ukraine	Kherson	283649	Cfa	25	64
Ukraine	Simferopol	336460	Cfb	24	94
Ukraine	Zaporizhzhya	710052	Dfa	23	69
Ukraine	Mykolayiv	470011	Dfa	27	90
Ukraine	Kyiv	2797553	Dfb	21	91
Ukraine	Kharkiv	1433886	Dfb	17	94
UK	London	8961989	Cfb	31	77
UK	Birmingham	1144919	Cfb	30	75
USA	Denver	715522	BSk	18	92
USA	Phoenix	1608139	BWh	42	114
USA	New York City	8804190	Cfa	26	89
USA	Houston	2304580	Cfa	41	96
USA	Los Angeles	3898747	Csb	44	91
USA	San Jose	1026908	Csb	41	93
USA	Chicago	2696555	Dfa	14	91
Uruguay	Montevideo	1270737	Cfa	37	87
Uruguay	Salto	99823	Cfa	33	95
Uruguay	Maldonado	55478	Cfb	44	84
Uruguay	San Carlos	27471	Cfb	44	84
Zambia	Mongu	52534	Aw	51	98
Zambia	Kawambwa	20589	Aw	52	89
Zambia	Livingstone	109203	BSh	47	98
Zambia	Lusaka	1267440	Cwa	53	97
Zambia	Ndola	451246	Cwa	49	91

THE STATISTICS

AVG_TEMP	PRECIP	PRECIP_DAYS	MAX_SNOW	SNOW_DAYS	MAX_DAY_HRS	LATITUDE	LONGITUDE
70	4.1	32	0	0	14.3	34.42	8.78
69	10.6	87	0	0	14.5	36.82	10.17
68	15.6	125	0	0	14.6	37.27	9.87
71	51.8	316	0	0	12	0.32	32.58
71	58.4	310	0	0	12	0.44	33.2
74	50.5	294	0	0	12	0.06	32.48
72	50.6	281	0	0	12	0.47	34.09
75	40	232	0	0	12.2	2.77	32.3
75	38	231	0	0	12.1	2.25	32.9
65	35.9	250	0	0	12.1	-1.25	29.99
56	13.1	112	0.4	1	15.6	46.64	32.61
57	19.2	124	7.5	9	15.4	44.96	34.11
55	13.6	119	0	0	15.8	47.85	35.12
55	15.3	110	0	0	15.7	46.98	31.99
52	24.4	154	4.3	41	16.2	50.45	30.52
52	14.2	130	5.5	53	16.1	49.98	36.25
52	28.7	211	0	0	16.4	51.51	-0.13
51	32.8	207	0	0	16.6	52.48	-1.9
52	14.4	113	0	0	14.8	39.74	-104.98
77	4.6	29	0	0	14.2	33.45	-112.07
58	44.6	159	3.9	15	14.9	40.71	-74.01
72	56.1	183	0	0	13.9	29.76	-95.36
63	12.4	42	0	0	14.3	34.05	-118.24
62	22.4	64	0	0	14.6	37.34	-121.89
56	42.4	118	11	22	15	41.85	-87.65
62	35.2	147	0	0	14.3	-34.9	-56.19
66	65.8	148	0.4	1	14	-31.38	-57.97
63	31.9	138	0	0	14.3	-34.9	-54.95
63	31.9	138	0	0	14.3	-34.79	-54.92
76	16.8	104	0	0	12.9	-15.25	23.13
69	46.9	190	0	0	12.6	-9.79	29.08
77	13.2	73	0	0	13.1	-17.84	25.85
77	0	0	0	0	12.9	-15.41	28.29
73	0	0	0	0	12.8	-12.96	28.64

CHAPTER 4

Your Scouting Visit

"And suddenly you know: It's time to start something new and trust in the magic of beginnings."

— Meister Eckhardt
Theologian, 12th Century CE

You're not planning to move somewhere without a visit, are you? If you become serious about a particular country based on the information you collect, you will need to spend some time there before making a decision. You'll be able to talk to real estate agents, expats, and, if appropriate, immigration lawyers, and check out the climate and scenery. Some expert expats recommend visiting twice, in two different seasons. But we're leaving because the house is already on fire, so you have a decision to make about that.

Please be sure to check your health insurance first!

TRAVEL DOCUMENTS

Will you need a visa for your visit? To prevent possible bankruptcy, you will need health insurance valid in the countries where you travel. (I'm shoehorning this in here again because it's important.)

So, will you need a visa for your visit? A US passport is all that's necessary to enter almost any country for 60 or 90 days. However, we can't count on that always being true. It might not be a coincidence that Brazil has started to require visas for US citizens in April 2025, just a couple of weeks after the US slapped a tariff increase on Brazil's exports. Note that *all travelers* will need an online "pre-clearance" from the European Travel Information and Authorization System (ETIAS) beginning... sometime, but it's been postponed until at least 2026. It's not *permission* to enter—just a way to keep tabs on you if you do enter. Almost everywhere, beyond 90 days, you will either need to renew your tourist visa (which is possible in some countries) or obtain some sort of longer-term visa. Every country has its own schemes.

Technically, "don't need a visa" may mean just that a free 60- or 90-day tourist visa is routinely stamped into your passport when you pass through passport control. In many countries, it is possible to renew it by crossing the border and returning in 24 hours (or even 15 minutes). Since the 29 European countries in the Schengen Area have open borders among themselves, you are free to travel through most of Europe once in the Area. In any country, the officers at the border have the discretion to deny entry upon arrival. If you've got something insulting about the king tattooed on your forehead, that's a felony in Thailand. It's a crime of fashion anywhere.

Hopefully, I do not need to tell you that overstaying your visa is always a bad idea, but especially if you want to have another visa in the future.

HEALTH INSURANCE

Am I repeating myself? Not taking care of this could lead to financial ruin. One of the saddest and most easily avoidable stories I ever heard was about a retiree attending a destination wedding overseas. She had a heart attack! She was not allowed to leave the country until she paid her hospital bill. She had to max out her credit cards. It cost her a substantial chunk of her retirement nest egg and put a big crimp on her golden years. Guess what: She thought she was covered. The whole situation could have been avoided or mitigated by spending $100 or so on travel insurance.

If you are working for a large international corporation, you may be in good shape—*or not,* if you are not on company business. Some plans may cover an emergency room visit only—*or not!* If you are covered by Medicare, you are out of luck. Approach this subject with diligence and press your insurer for details. Call your insurer, twice... ask for a supervisor. I was told by one customer service agent that I had overseas coverage, but I'd have to pay up front and wait for reimbursement. When I called again, I was told that I had coverage only for an emergency room visit. Be sure you are covered for evacuation. You *cannot* buy a policy once you leave the US, and you must generally pay your premium before or shortly after you book your first flight.

Even though you can buy online, this might be a good time to pick up the phone and call an agent who represents more than one company. They can help you get the coverage you need. Ask about any pre-existing conditions or other special situations. These policies are not subject to ACA rules. If you're also concerned about trip interruption, lost bags, and the like, you can buy insurance for that, usually rolled into some sort of medical coverage. I personally feel that I can self-insure for my bags and airfares. You can typically buy "trip insurance" as part of your ticket purchase, but not at a good price. It's a better option than kicking the can down the road until you can't buy the policy, though, or can't get coverage for your pre-existing conditions. I currently have an annual "trekker" health insurance policy that requires me to return to the US for a day or two every 70 days. This will not be the right thing once I formally migrate to Mysteria.

LODGING

You are not on vacation on your scouting trip, at least not all the time. Even if you are not ready to connect with a real estate agent, you will want to get a realistic picture of the sort of place where you might live. If you are like most of us, this is not a luxury hotel. On the other hand, I personally pretend to be a student backpacker sometimes, and I stay in cheap accommodations that I wouldn't want to live in indefinitely. On my recent trip, I stayed in cheap Airbnbs with a luxury hotel sprinkled in from time to time. Then I realized that a better strategy was to find an attractive Airbnb room in a home in an attractive neighborhood that I might like to live in. Your host might be willing to discuss the price of their home and offer to put you in touch with an agent friend. Trying out more than one neighborhood is a good idea. In a large city or popular expat destination, you should be able to find information about different neighborhoods.

In some countries, there are no multiple listing services like we have in the US, but property is still advertised on websites. Even if you choose not to meet with a real estate agent, you can get some ideas about the local market. If you do meet with an agent, someone who has experience with representing foreigners is best. The process is likely to be very different and inherently more complicated.

CURRENCY

If you haven't traveled much… it's true what you heard: They have different money! It's not all green, and it has women on it! And different sizes!

You will get a good exchange rate for foreign currency at your local bank or credit union in the US before you leave home. Call ahead, because your branch may need to order it from another branch or the mother ship. A bank will probably charge a fee, but a credit union may not. You will be able to buy euros or sterling or yen, but probably not Malaysian ringgits. It would be nice to have a bit of local cash when you arrive, but you don't want to be worrying about hundreds of dollars' worth.

The next option you will encounter is an exchange agency in an airport. Take a tip from singer Dionne Warwick: *Walk On By*! If you tried, you couldn't find a worse rate from a hotel concierge!

Your next option will be an ATM in the airport. VISA cards seem to be most widely accepted. Now you have another no-brainer choice. You can either have the local bank convert the amount to dollars, or you can let your US bank do it later. If you use the foreign bank, the ATM will tell you the exchange rate immediately. If you leave it to your home team, you will not know the rate, but it is certain to be lower. It's a rare case when you're better off taking the pig in the poke.

What about credit cards? You will face a similar choice. Charge in local currency and let your American friends convert.

In European countries, you will be all but *required* to use a credit card (although I had to have a cabbie drive me to an ATM in Northern Ireland a couple of years ago. I guess they're not European since Brexit.) In poorer countries, you will be able to use credit cards only in upscale places, and even there, they may tack on a fee.

I looked it up: Traveler's checks (*traveller's cheques, excusez-moi!*) still exist! If I'm not mistaken, I haven't bought one since the 1990s. I remember finding some old ones and having trouble cashing them at a bank *that sold the same checks* because the teller didn't know what they were.

LOCAL ATTITUDES TOWARD EXPATS

I was a little anxious about possible heated discussions or even insults in the street while traveling in Europe or Latin America. I even bought some "Elbows Up" t-shirts to pass as Canadian while travelling so I could truthfully say "He's just terrible for Canada" and be done. What actually happened: Nobody expressed any animosity to my American persona. As cabbies do, a couple of them brought up Trump after telling me about the beauty of the local girls. Once in Latin America, I passed two women of a certain age (mine) while crossing a bridge. After I'd gone five yards further, I heard one shout "Gringo!" behind me. I turned around and said "Sí?" She smiled, waved at me, and said in English, "How are you? Have a good day!" (I found everyone in this country to be very friendly and helpful. I can't begin to list all the ways.) As for my Canadian t-shirts, I got a half-dozen or so random thumbs-ups on the street. In some European capitals, it's tourists they're tired of, not Americans *per se*. I assume you understand that Frank Sinatra's *Three Coins in the Fountain* is not an invitation to spend your penny there. Don't fret about being American. Fret about being a tourist.

On the other hand, many locals do feel some resentment about foreigners buying up properties in resort areas and, in some cases, turning them into Airbnbs for foreign tourists. This has driven up housing and other prices for locals. In a Guatemalan tourist town, I recently paid about $3 for a haircut. In the town where my NGO operates, it was only $1.50. Both sound insignificant to an American. But put yourself in the shoes of a poor local facing doubling prices for necessities like haircuts, moto-taxis, bottled water, and so on. This phenomenon is not limited to poor countries. The situation is similar in "beachy" European communities, where well-off Americans, Britons, Europeans, and Asians are settling. I have a friend in Mysteria who is excited about my decision to move there, but she expressed the wish that I tell no Americans that I'm liking it! Ask your Airbnb hosts and others for their frank opinions on the subject and ask what you can do to make yourself more welcome (for example, learn the language or volunteer).

Of course, you also have the option exercised by a substantial fraction of expats. You can find an expat bubble that makes you happy and live inside it. I attended a conference for potential expat retirees once and was frankly shocked to learn how many wanted to spend their golden years pickling their livers on the beach. *Chacun à son goût,* I guess. No offense, but no thanks. But this book isn't about the best ways to spend your retirement.

CHAPTER 5

When You Like What You See

"The people of this country are ready to move again."

— Ronald Reagan
40th US President, 1911–2004

Now that you've found your new home, there's the paperwork and a lot of other practicalities. Many of the practicalities are the same as in the US, like getting your water turned on. But predictably, many are unique to moving to a foreign country.

RESIDENCE AND CITIZENSHIP

After a short period, your tourist visa will expire. You will need some kind of residence visa. It's a very complicated topic, and I can only speak in generalities. Before you make a commitment, you may want to consult with an immigration lawyer in your destination country. There are also agencies with sizeable teams and admirable track records that will lead you through the entire process. Of course, they don't do it gratis, and it may theoretically be possible to handle much of the paperwork on your own, but if you make a mistake, you could set things back for months and end up hiring an agency to complete the process you bungled.

PERPETUAL TOURISM

You won't need residency if you're particularly adventurous and have passive income or remote work. You could just be a nomad and move on every time your tourist visa expires. Singles and couples of all ages have done this for extended periods, and some wrote books about it. Of course, you will probably not be able to work legally. I'm a rule follower, but many countries do have a large informal economy in which you could probably hide for the length of a 90-day visa. Of course, the minimum penalty for getting caught is probably expulsion with an attention-grabbing stamp in your passport. Four years of nomadism might be enough to escape Trumpism, or you may even discover your perfect home during your travels. Nomadism is an attractive life for some.

RETIREMENT VISAS

Many countries have special visas for "retirees." A retiree is not necessarily an oldster. It's a matter of money: Will you have to work, or do you have enough passive income? (Passive income consists of rents from real estate, dividends, pensions, etc.) The income could come from the US or, in most cases, investment in your new home country. Typically, you must document that you have sufficient passive income to support yourself (which is typically not that much: $1,000–$3,000 per month, even in

Europe). The more important question is whether you can truly live on the passive income you have in the country you are interested in.

In some countries, you *can* work as long as you also have sufficient *passive* income to support yourself. (In other words, you can work as long as you don't really need to.) At the other end of the spectrum, in one country, you could decide in a year to open a bar in your beach town and hire workers, but *you couldn't work at your own bar* even though you could receive the bar's profits—that's passive. (Almost every country likes a job creator!) Generally, you can leave the country and return when you wish, subject to a minimum residence requirement. These visas are referred to as *pensionado* visas in Latin America and "passive income visas" elsewhere.

DIGITAL NOMAD VISAS

These visas are for prospective residents who work, but only remotely with clients outside the country. Digital nomads may need to show history of their active income, and the requirement may be higher than the income required for a retirement visa, since active income varies more than passive income.

INVESTOR ("GOLDEN") VISAS

Golden visa programs allow foreigners to obtain residence by investing. The amount of the investment varies by country and often by type of investment. In some countries, the investment can be the purchase of a home. In one country, a $200,000 investment is required, but $100,000 will suffice if invested in teak reforestation. It's more like $550,000 in a popular European destination. While some countries are creating new golden visa programs, others are increasing requirements. As mentioned previously, in countries with housing shortages, resentment has been accumulating against golden visa holders who buy properties and make them inaccessible to locals. Some countries are eliminating real estate as an investment option. But in other countries, investors can be absentee landlords and be present in the country only weeks or even days per year.

PERMANENT RESIDENCE WITH PERMISSION TO WORK

As you might have noticed, retirement and digital nomad visas depend on proof of income. To immigrate to work, a country will want you to prove that you have skills needed in the country. This is analogous to a "green card" and is usually the hardest way to gain residence, administratively speaking.

CITIZENSHIP

You may want to move on to citizenship from residence. Three to seven years is typical. Some countries value what I'll call "cultural integrity," and it's not much more than theoretically possible to become a citizen, except perhaps by "marrying into the family."

However, many countries offer citizenship by descent. For example, if you have one Irish-born grandparent (including in Northern Ireland), you *already are* a citizen of the Republic of Ireland. You only need to document the relevant births and marriages. In Italy and Germany, it's a lot more complicated (and there are more complicated possibilities in Ireland, too).

On the other hand, if you are concerned about citizenship for your children, you should be aware that almost every country in the Western Hemisphere grants birthright citizenship—

automatic for children born in the country—and almost no country in the Eastern Hemisphere does.

Some expats find it useful to acquire a second passport. Historically, the US has not been a big fan of dual nationality, but things are more easygoing these days. As mentioned, a US passport will currently get you into almost any country without a visa. But Brazil recently instituted a visa policy for Americans, and other countries could follow suit as US foreign relations get frostier. An EU passport is highly esteemed for the doors it opens. Most EU citizens can enter China without a visa for 30 days, whereas US citizens can enter for only 10 days visa-free. If things get *really* bad, a second passport might be your only ticket *out* of a country sometime. Who knows what may happen if that Trumpster Fire burns all US bridges to the EU and NATO, for example? (I guess Canada is a test case.)

A ROOF OVER YOUR HEAD

Now you need a crib. Some countries require evidence that you have purchased a home or signed a lease to issue a long-term visa.

Buying is a complicated topic because the legalities of land holding are different in different countries. Americans are used to holding property in *fee simple absolute*, meaning… it's all yours. You might be shocked to learn that Scotland dismantled feudal landholding only in 2000. (And no more thirlage! Look it up.) There may be special restrictions on foreign ownership of land, and it may be difficult to be sure your title is clear. To build a beach house in some countries, you may have to build it on land leased from the government long term. (The fancy term is "emphyteutic lease.")

In some countries, real estate agents are not licensed. In any country, it's important to find reputable agents and lawyers who know how to explain things to you. It's probably not a bad idea to rent for at least six months before buying.

BANKING AND TAXES

You're going to need a local bank account in most countries. (However, the US dollar is the official currency in Ecuador and El Salvador, and practically so in Belize and Panama.) It's likely that you will need to grant power of attorney to someone in the country. As with many other topics, bank policies vary from country to country and can't easily be summarized in a spreadsheet

Many American citizens living abroad are not in compliance with the IRS because they don't know that *every US citizen living abroad is required to file an income tax return*—even the ones that owe no taxes. You must also pay any income taxes in the country where you reside. You can't hide anything in a Swiss bank account anymore. The IRS receives reports from nearly every bank in the world, and you are required to report foreign bank accounts on your tax return. There is no statute of limitations on failure to file—none. Don't forget your liabilities to any US State. It may take some work to relinquish residency in your state to avoid taxes.

Because of differing treaty arrangements, filing US taxes is a little bit different in every country. Maybe you think you can do your own filings because you are just a humble 1040-EZ retiree receiving money from Social Security and IRA distributions. My situation is not much more than this, but when I move to Mysteria, you can bet I will hire a tax professional who specializes in helping expats for the first year at least.

You can't avoid death and taxes, but there is a radical way to avoid *US* taxes: renounce your citizenship after you obtain citizenship in another country. Surprise: The State Department can deny your request. If you haven't been filing your returns, your request won't be approved until you take care of the filings and pay any taxes you owe, with interest and probably fines. You could even be forced to raise cash to pay taxes on unrealized capital gains on illiquid assets. You will lose *all* advantages of US citizenship, but you still may not shed all the obligations. Very few people consider this option seriously, and with good reason. This door does *not* open in the other direction.

Source:

- *U.S. Taxes for Worldly Americans* by Olivier Wagner, 9th ed, 2025.

Conclusion

"I am a citizen of the world."

— Diogenes of Sinope
Greek Cynic Philosopher , Third Century BCE

Our house gets smokier every day.

Will Donald Trump choke on his own smoke?

Possibly, Republican politicians will start holding town meetings again and hear about how the Trump Administration is devastating their districts and finally take action. Possibly, Republicans will be swept out of office in 2026, and Democrats will impeach and remove him. Possibly, he will die of natural causes. What's the best we can hope for? Will we even *have* elections in 2026? It's really a grim picture. In 2024, DJT told a group of evangelicals that, if they voted for him in 2024, they'd never have to vote again. He has already released his J6 Brown Shirts, and they have already exhibited their willingness to assassinate Democratic leadership. Republicans continue to gerrymander congressional districts to their own advantage, discarding long-standing tradition to redraw boundaries only after the decennial census—Republicans at the state level who have gerrymandered their own districts as well. Will the President simply suspend elections in 2026, with the approval of the Supreme Court? One Justice recently said that the Trump Administration has the Court "on speed dial."

If Trump is removed from office, either politically or by his passing, what can we expect from JD Vance? If DJT is impeached, possibly Vance will be as well, or—since he likes to be a tick on the biggest dog—he might become a Democrat! But if Donald Trump drops dead, Vance and Republicans may see no reason to change course.

If the fire is put out and the smoke dissipates, it will take years to undo the damage. No one in the world considers the United States a reliable partner any longer—not just because Donald Trump and the GOP are unreliable, but also because a people that could elect him to the Presidency of the United States is itself inherently unreliable. And it will be excruciatingly difficult to repopulate the departments and agencies destroyed by Elon Musk and DOGE to recreate functional services for citizens.

What about you and me? Perhaps in 2029, we will at least feel that it is *safe* to return to the United States, and we will want to return. No one knows the future.

But I'd like to end my book in a better mood than I started. If you have read the book, you are obviously deeply unhappy with our country's direction and want to leave. I'm preaching to the choir.

Moving to another country is a great opportunity even in good times. To be philosophical, it broadens the mind. But at a practical level, the weather could be nicer, the skiing could be better, the people could be friendlier, learning the language could be stimulating, the architecture and history could be fascinating, the food could be tastier, and the living could be less stressful.

Some of us never thought of leaving before the current crisis, but many of us have had the idea of living elsewhere in our heads for a long time, maybe even since childhood. Many of us just decided at some point that childhood dreams don't come true. Some of us may just feel plain scared. Possibly, the rest of us have been balancing ill-defined and poorly informed positives and negatives on scales and waiting for the positives to clearly outweigh the negatives. I hope you've been able to confidently put clear positives and negatives on the scales. The state of our country is worse than a disgrace, but perhaps there's a silver lining; perhaps that weight could tip our scales and lead us to pursue new, more rewarding lives in another country.

If you've found my book helpful, please give it a review on Amazon and elsewhere, and please recommend it to a friend. Would it be a good gift for a new college graduate plotting out their post-academic life? Also, please visit www.thompained. com and let me know what countries interest you most. I'm planning a series of longer climate reports on cities and towns in individual countries, according to interest, and I will update the spreadsheets as new information becomes available.

Here's hoping that we all go to our happy places soon!

Appendix

"Smoking is the leading cause of statistics."

— Liza Minelli
American Entertainer, 1946–present.

For the geekiest of my readers, this section presents the sources of the data in the tables and explains my subsequent analysis.

GOVERNMENT DATA

Columns: DEMOCRACY, LIBERTIES

These columns are derived from the *World Democracy Index 2024*, published by EIU ("The Economist Intelligence Unit," part of The Economist Group). EIU makes its money by providing corporations with reports on the business environment in different countries. It distributes the widely cited World Democracy Index to the public without charge. I've rounded their numeric scores into letter grades as follows:

EIU score for "overall democracy"	EIU category	Letter grade
≥9	Full democracy	A
≥8 but <9	Full democracy	A-
≥7 but <8	Flawed democracy	B
≥6 but <7	Flawed democracy	B-
≥5 but <6	Hybrid System	C
≥4 but <5	Hybrid system	C-
<4	Authoritarian Regimes	omitted

The Economist also publishes six subcategories, also scored on ten-point scales. I included only "Civil Liberties" and assigned letter grades in the same way.

Countries scoring below 40 are ranked "authoritarian," and I haven't included them anywhere in this book. That leaves 99 of 158 countries in the report. Fortunately, 85% of American non-military expats live in these countries. (You might guess that North Korea has the lowest score. Sadly, despite millions spent on "democracy building," Afghanistan ranks a full eight points lower.)

At the end of 2024, the United States ranked near the top of the "flawed democracies," at 78, between France and Belgium, but far behind the nine countries scoring 90 and above. We can expect a precipitous fall in 2025, of course.

Source:

- *Democracy Index 2024: What's wrong with representative democracy?* Economist Intelligence Unit, 2025.

LANGUAGE DATA

Columns: OFFICIAL_LANGUAGE, ENG_PROFICIENCY

Wikipedia defines "official language" as the one (or more) used in legislative assemblies. In a country with many indigenous groups, the government may give legal recognition to indigenous languages and provide primary education in them, but various ethnic groups and the bureaucracy may communicate in the former colonial language. In fact, many countries around the world recognize several languages. If there are more than two, two are given with a footnote.

It has been difficult to get a good handle on the percentage of the population that can speak English in the world's countries. I relied on the English Proficiency Index (EPI) produced by EF Education First, since all other available options appear to compare apples to oranges. The EPI compares apples to apples, but the apples are not chosen very scientifically. The EPI is based on a proficiency test that any English student around the world can choose to take online. Exactly why do students decide to take it? My hypothesis is that students who think they will do well take the exam. If a country's self-selected students do poorly on average, it suggests that it will be difficult to communicate with anyone in English. It would be useful to know how many test-takers there are in each country, but this is unavailable. I translated the scores into letter grades.[1] Generally, grades seem consistent with anecdotal evidence. Austria and Germany received 600 and 598 points, respectively, so Germany is the unhappy student who just missed an A. (Probably, we all remember that feeling.)

---

1   *Only four African countries that were never British colonies received F.*

SOURCES:

- ▸ "List of official languages by country and territory." Wikipedia, https://en.wikipedia.org/wiki/List_of_official_ languages_by_country_and_territory, accessed 25 April 2025.
- ▸ "EF English Proficiency Index." EF (Education First), https://www.ef.edu/epi/, accessed 25 April 2025.

PURCHASING POWER DATA

Column: PURCH_POWER

As you know by now, a dollar goes a lot further in a place like Mexico or another tourist destination where standards of living are generally lower.

It all hinges on the fact that the US dollar is one of the handful of very stable currencies favored for international trade. (That's at this moment in late April 2025. However, it has dropped in value 11% versus the euro since our new president took office, pursuing his economic policies literally with a vengeance. For the sake of argument, let's assume all is grand.) The dollar's stability itself has a monetary value. If you exchange a dollar for Guatemalan quetzales with the same purchasing power, you give away the value of its usefulness in international trade. If you were involved in international trade (as opposed to buying a Guatemalan dinner), you would demand to receive quetzales with *more* purchasing power than your dollars. As an international trading company, just how many quetzales do you need for hotels for executives on business trips? As an expat, however, you can buy exactly the amount of quetzales that you need at the same exchange rate and shop locally. Someone gave you extra quetzales for the stability of the dollars, but you can use the extra immediately to buy dinner. Economists separate purchasing power from stability using the "Purchasing Power Parity Dollar (PPP)." It currently takes about $0.13 to purchase a Guatemalan quetzal, but if you spend it in Guatemala, it will buy around $0.29 worth of local goods. A US dollar will buy $2.26 worth of local goods in Guatemala. This applies only to *local* goods. Imported goods may be quite a bit more expensive than in the US due to tariffs and shipping costs. If you insist on American products, you may find that your cost of living *rises.* Cars and gasoline are also expensive in many countries due to taxes.

Exchange rates and local currency values constantly change, so letter grades are given in Table I to smooth over these effects. Countries with inflation rates exceeding 20% were given an F based on the inherent instability of their economies. PPP estimates for the calculation were part of a large World Bank dataset. Exchange rates are accessible on many websites and were downloaded on April 24, 2025. The table below shows how letter grades were assigned on that day:

Purchasing Power range	Letter grade	Example
$0.7 <= PP < $1	D	Denmark, Ireland
$1.00 PP		US (by definition)
$1.00 <= PP < $1.25	C	France, Canada
$1.25 <= PP < $2.00	B	Uruguay, Latvia
PP >= $2.00	A	South Africa, Ecuador
Inflation > 20%	F	Argentina (249%)
<4	Authoritarian Regimes	omitted

I can't predict what the situation will be when you read this, but the current relative standings are likely to be helpful. If you want to accumulate foreign currency before you are eligible to open a bank account in a foreign country, you can do this in an account at a discount brokerage house. You can either buy and own euros (for example) or buy shares in funds that invest in euros. However, you won't be able to buy Malaysian ringgits (for example).

Column: PURCHASING POWER

SOURCES:

- ▸ "US dollar exchange rates table." X-Rates, https://www.x-rates.com/table/?from=USD&amount=1, accessed 25 April 2025.
- ▸ "PPP conversion factor, private consumption." World Bank Group, https://data.worldbank.org/indicator/PA.NUS.PRVT.PP, accessed 25 April 2025.

DEMOGRAPHIC DATA

Columns: POPN_1000s, URBAN_PCT, POP_SQ_MILE, POP_65_UP, EXPATS, and EXPATS_M_TO_F

According to *World Population Review*, there are 3.1 million non-military Americans living abroad, 2.6 million in our list of democracies. Twenty-seven percent live in Mexico; 9% in Canada. Although balanced overall, the ratio of males to females varies from country to country in surprising ways: 1.24 in Greece; 0.78 in Germany. Table I reports the expat population of every country in thousands, along with the male/female ratio (useful for singles, I guess). Naturally, expats are not uniformly spread across a country.

If you are a "senior," you might like to know how many others are getting the great discounts seniors get in many countries. (I dislike being called a "senior," but I like the Spanish equivalent less: "of the third age," i.e., walking on three.)

The expat statistics do *not* include military personnel. Japan's contingent of 55,000 is the largest. Seventy percent of US overseas personnel are in Japan, Germany, and South Korea.

SOURCES:

- "Population, total." World Bank Group, https://data.worldbank.org/indicator/SP.POP.TOTL, accessed 25 April 2025.
- "Urban population." World Bank Group, https://data.worldbank.org/indicator/SP.URB.TOTL, accessed 25 April 2025.
- "Population density." World Bank Group, https://data.worldbank.org/indicator/EN.POP.DNST, accessed 25 April 2025.
- "American expats by country, 2025." World Population Review, https://worldpopulationreview.com/country-rankings/american-expats-by-country, accessed 25 April 2025.
- "Where are US Military Members Stationed and Why?." USA Facts, https://usafacts.org/articles/where-are-us-military-members-stationed-and-why/, accessed 25 April 2025.

CLIMATE DATA

Columns:

Table I: KG_TROPICAL, KG_ARID, KG_TEMPERATE, KG_CONTINENTAL

Table II: KG_CLIMATE, MIN_TEMP, MAX_TEMP, AVG_ TEMP, PRECIP, PRECIP_DAYS, MAX_SNOW, SNOW_DAYS, MAX_DAY_HRS

It takes more than a few words to describe a country's climate, and, of course, a country can have many climates— even a small country, if it has mountains and a coastline. Fortunately, Wladimir Köppen devised a classification system for climates in 1884, modified by Rudolf Geiger in the mid-20th Century. I refer to this as the "KG System." It consists of five major categories, A–E, usually translated as "tropical, arid, temperate, continental, polar." Each of these is further divided into subcategories, about 20 in all.

The table of cities gives the assigned category for that city. Table I shows which of A, B, C, and D are in some *city* in that country. (Most countries have a mountaintop in the E-zone, but there is no city atop the Matterhorn, for example.) They are displayed in four separate columns for spreadsheet sorting, with As, Bs, Cs, and Ds for ease on the eyes.

The KG *sub*categories are given for the cities in Table II. The section on City Climate below describes KG in more detail. The technical definitions of the subcategories, based on temperature and precipitation, can be found in the relevant Wikipedia entry.

Temperature and precipitation statistics are derived from 366 daily records for 2024 retrieved from the Meteostat website.

Another important aspect of climate is day length, determined by latitude. Except for Hawaiians, Americans are used to long days in the summer and long nights in the winter.

In the tropics, days and nights are roughly equal year-round. Many are surprised that Rome is a wee bit north of Chicago, so most of Europe has a longer Midsummer's Day than most of the US. Day length is directly computed from latitude.

Sources:

- ▸ "Köppen climate classification.," Wikipedia, https://en.wikipedia.org/wiki/Köppen_climate_classification,accessed 25 April 2025.
- ▸ "Latitude and longitude finder." http://LatLong.net.
- ▸ "The Weather's Record Keeper." http://meteostat.net, accessed 1–5 May 2025 via Python API.

WELL-BEING AND DEVELOPMENT DATA

The United Nations groups countries into income categories as *high, upper middle, lower middle,* and *low.* I have translated these into A, B, C, and D.

The Human Capital Index 2020 attempted to measure how much "human capital"—knowledge, skills, and health—that babies born in 2020 would accumulate by age 18. Human capital "is a central driver of sustainable growth and poverty reduction" and is regarded as a key statistic by development economists. Japan scored 0.80; only Singapore scored higher (0.88). Letter grades were assigned using cutoffs of 0.70, 0.60, 0.50, and 0.40. The US squeaked into the A category with 0.701.

Life expectancy at birth is a good measure of a country's health. It has been rounded to whole years and stated numerically. The US ranks 34th at 77.4. Life expectancy is a full seven years longer in Japan. (Sadly, life expectancy still sits at 53 for babies born in Nigeria, despite its incredible natural resources.)

The number of physicians per 1,000 people is self-explanatory.

Columns: HUMAN_CAPITAL_INDEX, LIFE_EXPECTANCY, INCOME_LEVEL, HUMAN_DEVEL_INDEX, PHYSICIANS_PER_1000

SOURCES:

- "Physicians (per 1,000 people)." World Bank Group, https://data.worldbank.org/indicator/sh.med.phys.zs, accessed 25 April 2025.
- "Human Capital Index (HCI)." World Bank Group, https://data.worldbank.org/indicator/HD.HCI.OVRL, accessed 25 April 2025.
- "Life expectancy at birth (total)." World Bank Group, https://data.worldbank.org/indicator/SP.DYN.LE00.IN, accessed 25 April 2025.
- "Human Development Index (HCI)." United Nations Development Programme, https://hdr.undp.org/data-center/human-development-index#/indicies/HDI, accessed 25 April 2025.

SAFETY DATA

Columns: TRAFFIC_DEATHS_PER_100000, PHYS_PER_1000

With the exception of the summary of gun laws, these numbers come directly from the sources cited below.

Wikipedia's article contains a complex table. I focused on the third column, labeled "Personal Protection." Data in this column are tagged in HTML as "yes," "partial," "maybe," and "no," as described in Chapter 3.

Sources:

- "Mortality caused by road traffic injury (per 100,000 population)." World Bank Group, https://data.worldbank.org/indicator/SH.STA.TRAF.P5, accessed 25 April 2025.

- "Overview of gun laws by nation." Wikipedia, https://en.wikipedia.org/wiki/Overview_of_gun_laws_by_nation, accessed 25 April 2025.

- "Estimated number of civilian guns per capita by country." Wikipedia, https://en.wikipedia.org/wiki/Estimated_number_of_civilian_guns_per_capita_by_country, accessed 25 April 2025.

- "American Expats by Country." World Population Review, https://worldpopulationreview.com/country-rankings/american-expats-by-country accessed 9 October 2025.

- "Intentional Homicide (per 100,000 people)." World Bank Group, https://data.worldbank.org/indicator/VC.IHR.PSRC.P5, accessed 25 April 2025.

www.ingramcontent.com/pod-product-compliance
Lightning Source LLC
Chambersburg PA
CBHW060247030426
42335CB00014B/1623